DEMBÉLÉ

MATT & TOM OLDFIELD

ULTIMATE FOOTBALL HEROES

DEMBÉLÉ

FROM THE PLAYGROUND TO THE PITCH

DINO

First published in the UK in 2025 by Dino Books,
an imprint of Bonnier Books UK,
5th Floor, HYLO, 105 Bunhill Row,
London, EC1Y 8LZ
www.bonnierbooks.co.uk

X @UFHbooks
X @footieheroesbks
www.heroesfootball.com
www.bonnierbooks.co.uk

Text copyright © by Matt Oldfield Limited, 2025

1 3 5 7 9 10 8 6 4 2

All rights reserved. No part of this publication may be reproduced, stored in a retrieval system, or transmitted in any form or by any means, without the prior permission in writing of the publisher, nor be otherwise circulated in any form of binding or cover other than that in which it is published and without a similar condition including this condition being imposed on the subsequent purchaser.

Paperback ISBN: 978 1 80078 640 0
E-book ISBN: 978 1 78946 924 0

The authorised representative in the EEA is Bonnier Books UK (Ireland) Limited.
Registered office address: Floor 3, Block 3, Miesian Plaza
50–58 Baggot Street Lower,
Dublin 2, D02 Y754, Ireland.
compliance@bonnierbooks.ie

The views in this book are the author's own and the copyright, trademarks and names are that of their respective owners and are not intended to suggest endorsement, agreement, affiliation or otherwise of any kind.
This book is unofficial and unauthorised and is not
endorsed by or affiliated with Ousmane Dembélé.

A CIP catalogue record for this book is available from the British Library

Typeset by IDSUK (Data Connection) Ltd
Printed and bound in Great Britain by Clays Ltd, Elcograf S.p.A

For Noah, Nico, Arlo and Lila

ULTIMATE FOOTBALL HEROES

Matt Oldfield is a children's author focusing on the wonderful world of football. His other books include *Unbelievable Football* (winner of the 2020 Children's Sports Book of the Year) and the *Johnny Ball: Football Genius* series. In association with his writing, Matt also delivers writing workshops in schools.

Cover illustration by Dan Leydon.
To learn more about Dan, visit danleydon.com
To purchase his artwork visit etsy.com/shop/footynews
Or just follow him on X @danleydon

TABLE OF CONTENTS

ACKNOWLEDGEMENTS 9
CHAPTER 1 – **SPRINTING TO GLORY**. 11
CHAPTER 2 – **FEARLESS FATIMATA** 20
CHAPTER 3 – **MOUSTAPHA AND 'LA MADELEINE'** 25
CHAPTER 4 – **ALM ÉVREUX** 30
CHAPTER 5 – **PARADISE IN PARIS** 37
CHAPTER 6 – **TOURNAMENT TESTS** 42
CHAPTER 7 – **THE ROAD TO RENNES** 47
CHAPTER 8 – **PASSING EVERY TEST**. 52
CHAPTER 9 – **MIKAËL'S BIG PREDICTION** 56
CHAPTER 10 – **TWO-FOOTED MAGIC** 62
CHAPTER 11 – **THE DORTMUND DEAL AND THE PERFECT MENTOR** 67
CHAPTER 12 – **FRANCE'S TOP YOUNG TALENT** 75
CHAPTER 13 – **UP FOR THE CUP** 80

CHAPTER 14 – **BARCA AT ALL COSTS**	86
CHAPTER 15 – **INJURY SETBACKS**	91
CHAPTER 16 – **WARNING SIGNS**	98
CHAPTER 17 – **A WORLD CUP ROLLERCOASTER: PART I**	103
CHAPTER 18 – **LAUGHS WITH LEO**	111
CHAPTER 19 – **A GOAL TO REMEMBER**	116
CHAPTER 20 – **NEVER GIVE UP**	120
CHAPTER 21 – **CONVINCING CAMP NOU**	125
CHAPTER 22 – **A WORLD CUP ROLLERCOASTER: PART II**	130
CHAPTER 23 – **CHAMPIONS AGAIN**	135
CHAPTER 24 – **COMING HOME**	140
CHAPTER 25 – **EUROS MAGIC**	148
CHAPTER 26 – **THE 'FALSE NINE' AND THE TREBLE QUEST**	153
CHAPTER 27 – **CHASING NEW GOALS**	161
DEMBÉLÉ HONOURS	164
GREATEST MOMENTS	167
TEST YOUR KNOWLEDGE	170
PLAY LIKE YOUR HEROES	172

ACKNOWLEDGEMENTS

First of all I'd like to thank everyone at Bonnier Books for supporting me and for running the ever-expanding UFH ship so smoothly. Writing stories for the next generation of football fans is both an honour and a pleasure. Thanks also to my agent, Nick Walters, for helping to keep my dream job going, year after year.

Next up, an extra big cheer for all the teachers, booksellers and librarians who have championed these books, and, of course, for the readers. The success of this series is truly down to you.

Okay, onto friends and family. I wouldn't be writing this series if it wasn't for my brother Tom. I owe him so much and I'm very grateful for his belief in me as an author. I'm also very grateful to the rest of my family, especially Mel, Noah, Nico, and of course Mum and Dad. To my parents, I owe my biggest passions: football and books. They're a real inspiration for everything I do.

CHAPTER 1

SPRINTING TO GLORY

31 May 2025, Champions League Final,
Allianz Arena, Munich, Germany

Ousmane Dembélé was grinning as he walked into the team meeting room. You would have never known that he was about to play in the Champions League final against Inter Milan. But that was just Ousmane's style.

It didn't mean he was calm on the inside, though. This was a huge moment for Paris St. Germain – or PSG, for short – and he knew how long the club had been waiting to get their hands on the Champions League trophy. There had been some heartbreaking European nights over the last ten years, and a few of the current squad had been there and had experienced those horror moments.

Of course, lifting this trophy would change all that. Ousmane had heard the talk on TV throughout the season. The media liked to say that PSG had reached another level since Lionel Messi, Neymar and Kylian Mbappé had all left – or that it was now a team of stars, not a collection of superstars – but Ousmane didn't like to think that way.

It *was* a new era, though. He could admit that. PSG had different players and a different style, with manager Luis Enrique in just his second year at the club.

PSG had already won the French league and cup double earlier in the month, so the season was just missing one last highlight to seal an unforgettable Treble.

'We've still got unfinished business.' That was the message in every meeting, and all the players knew that winning the Champions League would make them heroes for life in Paris.

When Coach Enrique had finished going over the

game plan, Ousmane thought about the team's run of results to reach this final. He would never forget the feeling of scoring against Liverpool at Anfield, or setting up a key goal against Aston Villa.

It meant even more to Ousmane because he had grown up near Paris. Back then, he was a kid scrambling to get PSG tickets with his friends. Now he was a first-team star, and it was his shirt that thousands of fans would be wearing in the crowd. A lot had changed over the years.

Before falling asleep the night before, Ousmane thought about the experienced Inter team that stood in their way. The Italian club had fought hard to get this far, but he still felt good about PSG's chances with their match-winning talent all over the pitch:

Gianluigi Donnarumma, the giant goalie
Achraf Hakimi and Nuno Mendes, the flying full-backs
Marquinhos, captain and centre-back colossus
Vitinha, the midfield magician

DEMBÉLÉ

Khvicha Kvaratskhelia (Kvara) and Désiré Doué, the wing wizards
And Ousmane himself, of course

Ever since he could dribble a ball, Ousmane had been known for his attacking play. There were long highlight videos packed with his mazy dribbles and spectacular goals. But Coach Enrique had an extra job for Ousmane in the final – and, for this, he wouldn't have the ball at his feet.

'It's a simple plan really,' Coach Enrique explained. 'We're not giving Inter any time to get comfortable. They like to play the ball around at the back from goal kicks, so I want you leading the press from the edge of the box as soon as they touch the ball.'

The coaches showed a few clips on the big screen. Ousmane watched closely as Inter goalkeeper Yann Sommer tapped a short pass to one of his defenders inside the box.

'As soon as the ball is kicked, give us full-speed pressing,' Coach Enrique said. 'Sprint until they panic.'

Ousmane nodded. He understood the job.

'There's no one faster than Dembouz!' Achraf called out, using Ousmane's childhood nickname.

But it would take some practice to get it right.

'Wait, wait, go!' the coaches shouted as they worked on the drill in training. 'Sprint! That's it, Ousmane.'

Those instructions were still running through Ousmane's head as he put on his Number 10 shirt and walked out into the tunnel at Allianz Arena. These minutes always seemed to go by so slowly! It was like being back at school and waiting to go out for the lunchtime football match.

The roar of the crowd told him that it was finally showtime. The teammates in front of him were slowly moving forward, and he followed them, looking ahead to the glimpses of a green pitch. The atmosphere took his breath away. He had played at the World Cup and the European Championships, but this was up there with the biggest nights of his career so far.

Ousmane didn't have to wait long to be part of the action. On the first Inter goal kick, he stood on the white line that marked the edge of the penalty area and crouched into a sprinting position, like an athlete in the Olympic 100 metres final. An Inter defender looked at him in surprise, unsure what was happening.

As soon as Sommer played the usual short pass, Ousmane flew into the box like he was launched from a cannon. With four lightning steps, he was closing in on the ball – and Inter panicked, kicking the ball aimlessly up the pitch.

'Yes, Ousmane! Perfect!' the coaches yelled, giving him a thumbs up.

The rest of the first half was like a dream. Achraf made it 1–0 to finish off a quick team move, before Kvara floated a pass up the line to set Ousmane free on the left wing. The Inter defenders backed off, so Ousmane dribbled on. He curled a cross to Désiré, whose shot whistled into the net with the help of a deflection.

'Yeeeessssss!' Ousmane screamed, punching the air in delight. He ran over to celebrate with Désiré.

Inter didn't know what to do. Ousmane was soon back in position on the edge of the box. Again, he sprinted at full speed towards the Inter keeper and defenders, forcing a rushed pass. Another time, he almost blocked the clearance.

Behind him, he heard Vitinha and Kvara clapping his effort.

'Great work, Dembouz!' Vitinha shouted.

But Ousmane was still at his best when he was attacking. In the second half, PSG created more chances. Vitinha burst forward and slipped a pass to Ousmane. Without even glancing up, he knew what Vitinha was thinking. Ousmane fooled two Inter defenders with a genius back-heel into Vitinha's path for a killer one-two, leading to another beautiful goal for Doué. 3–0. It felt like the knockout blow.

Ten minutes later, Ousmane dropped deeper to get on the ball and spotted Kvara racing ahead of his marker. No one was tracking the run. Ousmane's pass was perfectly placed, and Kvara smashed a shot into the net. 4–0.

Now even the PSG subs were running to the corner flag to celebrate. The party had begun.

'What a pass!' Kvara shouted, hugging Ousmane and lifting him off the ground.

Ousmane smiled and encouraged his teammates to keep attacking. 'We want five!' he called to Vitinha when PSG won another corner.

Substitute Senny Mayulu smashed in a fifth goal just before full-time, and PSG's 5–0 victory became the biggest ever win in a Champions League final. Ousmane wasn't thinking about the history books, though. He wanted to get his hands on the trophy, which soon appeared with red and blue ribbons on the handles.

'I love this team!' he yelled as the size of their achievement sunk in.

Ousmane walked up behind Coach Enrique to get his medal. Then he huddled with his teammates on the podium while Marquinhos appeared with the trophy.

'Whoooooooooaaaaaaaa… Hurraaaaaaaaay!' they all screamed.

Campeones, Campeones, Olé! Olé! Olé!

Ousmane had played in enough big games to know what this night meant. Even the greatest teams rarely saved their best football for the biggest games, but that was exactly what Ousmane and PSG had done.

As Ousmane waved to his family and friends in the crowd, his smile widened. They deserved to be wearing this winner's medal too, and he knew that he would never have reached this moment without them.

CHAPTER 2

FEARLESS FATIMATA

Little Ousmane wriggled in his bed and tried to get comfortable. He felt tired, but somehow he was still awake. He rubbed his eyes and sat up.

His bedroom door was slightly open, and he could see faint light sneaking through. What time was it? It couldn't be the morning already.

Ousmane tiptoed into the hallway, dodging the old football that he liked to keep by the door. He saw his mum, Fatimata, sitting in a chair at the kitchen table, fixing a pair of his trousers that had a hole in the knee. That hole was the result of Ousmane's latest match outside with his friends.

Fatimata looked up in surprise when she heard his footsteps.

'Ousmane, it's really late!' she whispered. Everyone called him Ousmane, even though his full name was Masour Ousmane Dembélé. 'Did you have a nightmare?'

Ousmane shook his head. 'No, I just can't sleep,' he replied. 'I've tried everything.'

'Come here, little man,' she said gently. 'I thought you'd be exhausted after playing at the park this afternoon.'

With a smile, Ousmane weaved past a couple of chairs and sat next to his mum.

Fatimata folded the trousers and put them on the table. She scooped Ousmane up and lifted him onto her knee. He rested his head on her shoulder, and she began to hum a bedtime song she had learned years ago in Mauritania, before moving to France for a new life and new opportunities.

'When I was a little girl, this was my favourite lullaby,' she explained. 'Everyone used to sing it. It didn't matter how wide awake I was, this lullaby would always get me to sleep.'

'That must have been years and years ago!'

Ousmane said, giggling.

'Okay, cheeky, do you want to hear it or not?' Fatimata answered. She was giggling too.

'Yes, Mama! Please!' he said.

Fatimata switched from humming to singing, and Ousmane closed his eyes. His mum could be fierce and even a little scary when he was in trouble, but now he felt safe and calm.

A minute later, he was yawning. Two minutes later, he was snoring peacefully.

Fatimata smiled. 'The song still works!' she said to herself as she carried Ousmane back to his bed. She tucked him under his sheet and gave him a gentle kiss on his forehead.

As she sat down again at the table, she wished it could be bedtime for her too. But there were still jobs on her list before the start of another day. She had food to prepare, clothes to wash and bills to pay. Life wasn't easy, but Fatimata always found a way to get things done.

When she had finally finished her jobs, she peeked through the bedroom door to check on Ousmane and his little brother and sister. They were all counting on her, and she would never let them down.

'Time to sleep,' she said to herself, turning off the kitchen light. But at that same moment there was a little knock on the front door, almost too quiet to hear.

Fatimata opened the door cautiously. It was one of her neighbours – Zola, a mum with a little two-year-old girl.

'I'm sorry it's so late,' Zola said. 'My boss just called, and I have to work tomorrow night. Could you look after my daughter until I get home?'

Tomorrow was already going to be a busy day, with work and school, but Fatimata nodded. 'Of course, yes,' she replied. 'I'll be home by four o'clock so you can drop her off any time after that.'

That's what it meant to be a local community. They helped each other whenever they could, because a little kindness could make all the difference when nothing else seemed to be going right.

As Fatimata finally turned off the lights and brushed her teeth, she reminded herself that tomorrow was a new day. 'Be brave, be strong, be determined,' she said to herself, looking at her reflection in the mirror.

Even though he didn't realise it yet, Ousmane was picking up all those same qualities, following his mum's example. In the years ahead, he would need to be brave, strong and determined, on many occasions during his football journey.

CHAPTER 3

MOUSTAPHA AND 'LA MADELEINE'

Ousmane looked out of the window. The rain had stopped! He picked up his ball and rushed back into the kitchen.

'I'm going to get Moustapha!' he called to his mum. 'It's football time!'

'Some fresh air will do you good,' Fatimata agreed. 'But stay on this side of the road so I can see you from the window.'

Ousmane paused long enough to shout 'Okay!' and then he was scampering to Moustapha's front door. They lived in the same building called 'La Madeleine'. It was a tall block of flats in Évreux, less than two hours from Paris, the capital city of France, and

DEMBÉLÉ

Ousmane and Moustapha had been friends since the first time they played football together.

Moustapha was just as football crazy as Ousmane, and for both of them, any spare minute was a chance to work on their skills. One day, it was a competition for who could do the most keepy-ups. The next day, it was a penalty shootout. 'La Madeleine' had a concrete pitch, surrounded by a fence that made it feel like a cage, and Fatimata knew where to find Ousmane if he was late for supper.

'Ready to play?' Moustapha said, opening the door and putting on his trainers in such a hurry that he almost tripped.

'Let's do it!' Ousmane replied, spinning the ball in his hands.

When they stepped outside, they saw that three other friends were already there with the same idea. The pitch had a few little puddles but it would take more than that to cancel the evening match.

Five minutes later, a 5 v 5 game was underway, and Ousmane was a blur of movement. He was only six, but all the local kids knew about his skills. Some had direct experience of being embarrassed by his dribbling. Others had only heard the stories.

Tonight, he and Moustapha were on the same team, and the goals were flying in. It didn't even make a difference when one of the older boys took over as goalie.

'You could have three keepers and we'd still score!' Ousmane shouted, laughing and high-fiving Moustapha.

But these games felt like friendly kickabouts compared to the matches against the local neighbourhoods. Those were the biggest ones. Local pride was on the line, and Ousmane was ready to join in, even when most of the other players were at least two years older than him.

'This skinny kid is your secret weapon?' one of their opponents said. 'Seriously?'

'Good luck with that!' added another boy who was wearing a backwards cap on his head. 'Too easy!'

Ousmane just grinned. 'We'll see,' he said. He didn't mind being the underdog.

There wasn't a lot of space on the pitch, but he

made the most of what he could get. His eyes lit up when a shot deflected straight to him on the wing.

'Go on, Dembouz!' Muha shouted. 'Take him on! Cook him!'

With a quick dribbling run, Ousmane got past one defender and left two more trailing as he changed direction in a flash. He passed to Moustapha and kept running forward for a one-two. Ousmane reached Moustapha's flick just in time and poked a shot past the keeper.

Gooooooooooooooooooooooaaaaaaaaaaaaaaaaaaa aaaaaaalllllllllllllllllllllllllllll!

That seemed to silence their opponents temporarily. But Ousmane wasn't done yet. He was feeling so confident that he didn't hesitate when a ball looped up in front of him. He just swung his foot at it, arrowing a half-volley into the bottom corner.

Gooooooooooooooooooooooaaaaaaaaaaaaaaaaaaa aaaaaaalllllllllllllllllllllllllllll!

Now he was feeling good. 'You were right,' he told Backwards Cap Boy. 'It *was* too easy.'

A little crowd had gathered next to the fence on one

side of the pitch. They were all cheering for the boys from 'La Madeleine'. They won the game 5–2, and his teammates lifted Ousmane into the air.

'And here's today's Man of the Match,' Moustapha said, pretending to give Ousmane a trophy.

Sometimes, though, Ousmane's tricks got him in trouble with defenders, even when he was playing against his friends and they were going for a clean tackle. With his quick feet, one second the ball was there; the next second, it was gone.

On plenty of nights, he limped home, dreaming of lying down on his bed – and on plenty of nights, he winced as his mum cleaned his cuts and put on plasters.

The bumps and scrapes never kept Ousmane down for long, though. When the next match arrived, he was always ready to play.

CHAPTER 4

ALM ÉVREUX

'Ousmane!' Fatimata called. 'Come on, it's dark outside! Put the ball away!'

After their evening matches, the other boys usually went back inside. But Ousmane liked to stay on the pitch. He wanted to keep practising, and he often didn't even notice what time it was. He just took shot after shot at the empty net, imagining that famous keepers like Gianluigi Buffon and Iker Casillas were staring back at him. Left foot, then right foot, then left foot again.

Finally, Fatimata reached her limit with the late-night games, the cuts and the occasional broken windows. She needed a new plan for her son's football development.

'It's time for Ousmane to find a real team,' she told Zola while they sat on a bench at 'La Madeleine'. 'If they play on grass instead of concrete, that would be nice too!'

Fatimata didn't have to look far for an answer. ALM Évreux was a short walk from 'La Madeleine', and that was the club that two of her neighbours recommended.

Ousmane jumped out of his chair when he heard he would be joining a training session.

'Thank you, Mama!' he shouted, hugging her and rushing off to find his favourite T-shirt.

Ousmane wasn't really worried about whether he would be good enough to sign for ALM Évreux. Instead, as the training session got nearer, he started picturing what it would be like if Moustapha and the other boys from 'La Madeleine' joined the team too.

Later that week, ALM Évreux youth team coach Gregory Badoche was putting out cones ready for practice. He was also looking forward to meeting a new player. The boy's mum had made a strong case for a trial, and he was always interested in discovering good young players.

DEMBÉLÉ

A few of the other kids had arrived early, and Coach Badoche whistled for them to come over.

'We've got a new boy joining us today called Ousmane,' he said. 'He hasn't played for a club before, so make him feel welcome.'

Coach Badoche looked up as a boy strolled over. This must be Ousmane, he thought. He watched the body language of the boy, who looked like he had been playing football there for years.

'He's too skinny to survive in real games,' claimed Patrick, one of the assistant coaches, appearing next to him. 'It looks like a strong wind would blow him over.'

'Well, I asked one of the older boys about him yesterday,' Coach Badoche replied. 'He said Ousmane is the best dribbler he knows. I guess we'll find out now. Let's see what he can do.'

While Ousmane stood on the edge of the warm-up circle, Coach Badoche introduced him to the rest of the group. Ousmane recognised a few of the other boys from the neighbourhood games – a tall boy called Luc and a boy with long hair called Eric.

He could tell they remembered him too. He went back through his memories of those matches to see whether he had embarrassed any of them. He didn't think so.

After leading the boys through two laps of the pitch, Coach Badoche paired Ousmane with Luc for a passing drill, pointing to the cones where he wanted them to stand.

'Two touches!' Coach Badoche shouted. 'Control and pass.'

The boys pinged passes back and forth. Ousmane carefully cushioned each pass from Luc and then sent the ball back – sometimes with his right foot, sometimes with his left foot.

'Very nice, Ousmane!' Coach Badoche called. 'Boys, you should all be switching between your stronger foot and your weaker foot.'

At the water break, Ousmane jogged over to get his bottle.

'What do you think so far?' Luc asked.

'I feel like a real footballer,' Ousmane answered, grinning. 'I've never had a coach before.'

'I joined the team last year and I've learned so much already,' Luc said. 'If you love football, this is the place to be.'

It was definitely different from playing at 'La Madeleine'. Ousmane was used to the end-to-end flurry of action and solo runs on the concrete pitch, but here the coaches wanted to see quick passing and good positioning. It was all about playing as a team.

Ousmane was a quick learner, so he already had a plan. Why not take the best of both styles?

When Coach Badoche split them into two teams for a short game at the end of the session, Ousmane sensed his chance to show why he deserved to join the club.

'Okay, it's the moment you've all been waiting for,' Coach Badoche said. 'We'll finish with a game. The first team to score five goals wins.'

Ousmane started on the right wing. Most of the boys were crowded in the middle of the pitch, so he had lots of space. Luc poked a clearance up the line, and Ousmane sprinted to reach it.

One defender chased back, but Ousmane was too fast. Another defender slid in with a tackle but ended

up just kicking the air as Ousmane faked to go left
then weaved to the right.

'Wow, what a move!' Coach Badoche said quietly
on the touchline.

Now Ousmane's instinct was to keep dribbling and
take a shot. But that wasn't the ALM Évreux way, and
he had teammates calling for a pass. So he took the
unselfish option, slipping the ball through to Eric for
an easy finish.

The coaches were all paying attention now.

'He's so smooth with the ball,' Patrick admitted.
'That dribbling skill is really rare for a seven-year-old.'

'Oh, so you've changed your opinion now?'
Coach Badoche asked, reminding Patrick about his
earlier doubts.

'Well, that was before I knew he was a little
magician!' Patrick joked.

While the coaches huddled the players together
for some final instructions, Ousmane wasn't sure
what was next. Should he just go home now?
Was he allowed to come to the next ALM Évreux
practice as well?

Before Ousmane could think of his own answers to those questions, Coach Badoche appeared with a clipboard and some papers.

'Great work tonight, Ousmane,' he said. 'You're exactly the kind of player we're looking for, and we want to make it official. Here are the registration papers for your mum to fill out. Just bring them to the next practice, and that'll be everything we need. Welcome to the team!'

CHAPTER 5

PARADISE IN PARIS

When Ousmane turned the corner on his way home to 'La Madeleine' after a busy day at school, he expected to hear the usual noise coming from the football pitch. But today it was all quiet.

Where was everyone?

He didn't have to look far. Inside the building, the boys were all crowded together. Ousmane weaved through a little gap to get close enough to hear what was going on.

'So, we'll leave on Saturday morning at ten, and then there are two options for the train,' one of the older boys was explaining. 'Let me know by tomorrow if you're coming.'

Ousmane looked over at Moustapha for some

clues, but his friend was just grinning and hopping with excitement. Muha, another football regular, was no help either.

'I can't believe this!' Muha said loudly. 'This is going to be amazing!'

Ousmane couldn't bear it any longer. 'What can't you believe? What's going to be amazing?' he asked desperately.

Moustapha came to the rescue. 'They're organising a trip to Paris to see PSG at the Parc des Princes stadium!'

'What?!!!!' Ousmane screamed.

Moustapha and Muha laughed. 'That was our reaction too!' Muha said.

But Ousmane knew there was something else he needed to do before he could really get excited. He had to speak to his mum.

He spent a few minutes thinking about the best moment to ask her, but then he gave that up. He knew he wouldn't be able to keep this news to himself for long anyway.

He ran up the stairs, two at a time, and opened the

front door.

'Mama! Mama! I need to talk to you.'

Fatimata hurried to the door with a worried look on her face.

Ousmane held up his hand. 'Sorry, I'm okay, it's nothing bad,' he said, realising that his excitement probably sounded like panic to her.

Fatimata relaxed a little. 'So what's the problem?' she asked.

'Can I go to Paris on Saturday?' he asked, putting on his sweetest face. 'There's a PSG game, and Moustapha and the other boys are all going.'

Fatimata thought about it. 'Are any of the parents going? Which older boys will be there?'

Ousmane told her everything he knew about the outing.

'How are you going to pay for it?' Fatimata added. 'PSG tickets aren't cheap!'

'I'll use the birthday money I've saved,' Ousmane said. 'That would be the best present ever.'

'I can see you've thought of everything!' Fatimata said, smiling. She checked the plans with some of the other parents and then gave Ousmane the good news: 'If you promise to be responsible and stay with the older boys, you can go.'

Ousmane jumped in the air. 'Thank you!' he said, hugging his mum. 'I'll be on my best behaviour.'

He felt the excitement building from the minute he woke up on the day of the game, and he was totally speechless by the time they arrived at the stadium. It felt huge from the outside.

Ousmane showed his ticket to the woman at the gate, then followed the rest of the group as they climbed up to their seats.

There were still twenty minutes before kick-off, so a few of his friends hurried off to get snacks. 'Are you coming?' Moustapha asked, tapping Ousmane on the shoulder.

'No, I'm staying here,' Ousmane said. Nothing was going to get him out of his seat now. The warm-up had just started, and he was watching every touch. He could see two of PSG's strikers, Pauleta and Peguy Luyindula, and winger Jérôme Rothen.

'This is football paradise!' he whispered to himself.

The noise in the stadium was already really loud, and it grew even louder when the game kicked off. Soon, Ousmane and his friends were joining in with all the PSG songs and pointing to all the flags and banners in the crowd. He tried to imagine what it would be like to walk down the tunnel and onto the pitch.

The match whizzed past faster than Ousmane wanted, but he felt lucky to be there as PSG put on a show, scoring three goals in an easy win.

'What a game!' Ousmane said as they left the stadium. He was still walking on air after seeing his football heroes up close.

'If you keep working on your killer moves, maybe you'll play on that pitch one day, Dembouz!' Moustapha replied.

Ousmane laughed. 'I've got a lot of work to do first,' he said. 'But don't worry, if I get there, I'll be sure to save you a ticket.'

CHAPTER 6

TOURNAMENT TESTS

It didn't take long for Ousmane to become ALM Évreux's biggest star. He was breaking records and getting better every week. Even when he had scored a hat-trick in the last game, he came back hungry to do it again. By now, Moustapha and Muha had joined the team too, and they were recreating their magic from games at 'La Madeleine'.

'We can beat anyone when we play like that!' Ousmane said after they crushed a league rival 4–1.

'Well, you'll get the chance to prove that this summer,' Coach Badoche replied mysteriously.

The ALM Évreux players looked round at him. 'What do you mean, Coach?' they said, all at once.

'I was going to wait until later to tell you, but

there's going to be a tournament this summer, and I've entered us in it,' he explained. 'All the best local teams will be there.'

That became the big target for all the boys and a reason to work even harder in training. Ousmane started staying for extra shooting practice and soon his teammates were doing the same.

There was a buzz on the bus as they travelled to the tournament. When they arrived, he saw some teams they recognised, and others who had travelled much longer distances. In their red-and-black kits, ALM Évreux showed no fear, scoring some spectacular goals and defending bravely.

Even when they weren't playing, there was still only one topic of conversation: football.

'Who's your favourite team?' Eric asked Ousmane one afternoon.

'I like watching Liverpool and Manchester United,' he replied.

'Aren't they rivals?!' Moustapha asked, laughing.

'Well, how am I supposed to choose?' Ousmane answered. 'David Beckham was one of my favourite players when he was at United. His free kicks were unstoppable! But Steven Gerrard is so good too, and Liverpool are amazing in the Champions League.'

'I prefer Rooney,' Muha interrupted. 'That boy has style!'

'I don't understand how England haven't won a big tournament with all these great players,' Ousmane said, shaking his head. 'It doesn't make sense.'

Moustapha laughed. 'You guys know you're supposed to support France, right?'

'I do support France!' Ousmane fired back. 'But I'm an England fan boy as well!'

Ousmane loved the laughs and the jokes, but he turned serious whenever there was a tournament game to win. ALM Évreux got through to the final, and he walked past the table with the trophy and the medals while waiting for the big match.

'It's time to start my trophy collection,' he thought to himself.

Big players show up in big games. Ousmane remembered hearing that on TV during the last World Cup. Well, this definitely counted as a big game for him.

But there weren't many chances in a tight first half. Moustapha made two good blocks, and Ousmane fired his only shot just wide.

'Keep battling!' Coach Badoche told them as they all guzzled water. 'When we win the ball back, let's move it faster. Give Ousmane a chance to attack before they get all their defenders in position.'

Finally, a long clearance gave Ousmane space to run. He sped away from his marker and cut inside onto his right foot. He glanced to his right and none of his teammates had caught up with him. He was on his own.

Ousmane dribbled on, with two quick stepovers. That made the last defender back off a little, just as Ousmane had hoped. Now he could see the goal, and the keeper was a little out of position. Before anyone knew what was happening, Ousmane curled a quick shot towards the far corner. The keeper reacted too late, and his dive got nowhere near the ball.

Goooooooooooooooooooooaaaaaaaaaaaaaaaaaa aaaaaaalllllllllllllllllllllllllllll!

Even Ousmane was a little surprised to see the shot sneak into the net.

DEMBÉLÉ

'Demboooooooooooouz!' Moustapha screamed, jumping on his back. 'You're the man!'

ALM Évreux just had to defend now. There couldn't be many minutes left. Ousmane could feel his legs aching, but he kept running. He thought about Beckham and Gerrard. They always found an extra burst of energy.

At last, Ousmane heard the final whistle. He was still hunched over, trying to catch his breath, when his teammates piled around him. What a feeling!

He shook hands with the other team and the tournament organisers, then collected his medal. He put it round his neck and held it up to get a better look.

'I could get used to this!' he said while the players stood together in front of one of the nets. They were almost too tired to smile for the photo.

'Great goal, Ousmane!' Coach Badoche said, putting his arm round Ousmane. 'Look after that medal. I have a feeling it'll be the first of many medals for you in the years ahead!'

CHAPTER 7

THE ROAD TO RENNES

Ousmane had enjoyed being the underestimated football star at 'La Madeleine' and the unknown wonderkid for ALM Évreux, but he wasn't a secret anymore. Things were getting serious.

Top academies across the country were tracking Ousmane now, and it had become normal for a group of scouts to show up at ALM Évreux youth team matches.

'Just focus on playing your game,' Coach Badoche kept reminding Ousmane. 'Block out everything else.'

Ousmane had been trying to do that, but it was difficult to ignore all the sudden attention. It was a lot for a twelve-year-old to handle. The scouts all wanted to meet him and his family, ask him questions and tell him about their youth teams.

After the latest game, Ousmane shook hands with three scouts – one from Caen, one from Rennes and one from Le Havre. When his teammates walked past, they couldn't resist the chance to tease Ousmane.

'Here's the star man!' Moustapha called loudly. 'Sign him up before it's too late!'

'Ousmane, can I have your autograph?' Muha asked, laughing.

Ousmane waved them away, but he appreciated the distraction. He was at his happiest when he was on the pitch with his teammates. In a lot of ways, he didn't want anything to change.

But it was also exciting to be wanted by teams in France's top division. Ousmane listened to all the details. Each club's football facilities sounded great, but there was one other key question on his mind – and it had nothing to do with football. *Would he have to move away from his family?*

Fatimata was determined to get that answer.

'If my son is leaving home, I need to understand exactly where he's going and how he will be looked after,' she said.

This was a whole new world for her, but she wanted to help Ousmane make the right decision.

'Why should Ousmane sign for you?' she asked each of the clubs.

There were lots of good answers, and all the scouts seemed to think Ousmane could rise quickly through the academy teams. Which club should he choose?

Sitting at the kitchen table, Ousmane tried to picture himself playing for each of the teams that were interested. An hour later, he was still just as confused.

'I don't know if I'm ready to make this kind of decision,' Ousmane admitted while he and Moustapha took turns shooting at the park. 'It's a decision that could change my whole life.'

'Are you asking me to feel sorry for you because so many big clubs want to sign you?' Moustapha joked. 'I mean, that does sound terrible!'

Ousmane laughed. 'Oh, come on – I know I'm very lucky to be in this position,' he said. 'I just never thought it would happen this quickly.'

'Trust your gut,' Moustapha said. 'You'll know

what to do.'

Rennes moved fastest to put together a plan. They understood that family really mattered to Ousmane and came up with a way for Fatimata and the rest of the family to move with him. That was reassuring, and Ousmane was ready to make his decision. He was going to sign for Rennes.

The excitement bubbled up for this new challenge, but it was still hard to say goodbye to his friends at 'La Madeleine', even though he knew he would be back to visit.

'This isn't really a goodbye,' he told Moustapha, giving him a high-five and a hug. 'It's just a see-you-soon.'

It was only really when Ousmane got to Rennes that he realised what this move meant. He was now a step closer to his dream of becoming a professional footballer with this youth team contract, and the setup at Rennes was so impressive.

'I think we made the right choice!' Ousmane whispered to his mum during their tour. 'Did you see how perfect the training pitches were?!'

It wasn't just the facilities that looked top class. The other youngsters in the Rennes academy were really good too. Ousmane knew he would have to work hard to keep up.

CHAPTER 8

PASSING EVERY TEST

Ousmane was quiet in his first few weeks while he adjusted to new teammates and a new coaching style, but he made a loud impression in training.

He was electric on the ball, dribbling at speed when defenders gave him too much space and tricking his way free when they got too close. The Rennes coaches exchanged looks on the touchline. They were all thinking the same thing: *this kid is destined for the first team.*

Vision and awareness were the next two hurdles for him. The coaches reminded him that he didn't have to go on a mazy run every time he got the ball. He became too predictable when he did that. Instead, he could mix his dribbling with a more direct style sometimes, or a more patient approach when Rennes were winning.

'The first thing is always to take a look,' one of the coaches explained. 'Get your head up so you have a picture of not just where the defenders are, but also where your teammates are. Otherwise, you might miss a striker unmarked in the box. A simple touch and a quick cross can be just as deadly as dribbling past three defenders. It's all about making the right decision.'

Ousmane nodded. He was thinking about a moment during his last game with the Under 15s when he had tried too many tricks. It was only when he lost the ball that he noticed there had been four Rennes players in the box waiting for a cross.

'I can do that,' he said. 'Even though I love going past defenders, it isn't always the best option.'

But the most common memory from those academy years was Ousmane getting it right – a screamer that flew into the top corner, a back-heel to fool a defender or a no-look pass that launched a counterattack. He set up so many goals. It didn't even matter that opponents were sometimes marking him with two or

DEMBÉLÉ

three players. When Rennes got the ball to Ousmane, something exciting usually followed.

Just like at 'La Madeleine', he tried to squeeze in every extra minute possible on the training pitch.

'Time to go home, Ousmane!' the coaches called. 'Even Messi and Ronaldo take a break sometimes!'

'Well, this is my chance to catch up with them, then!' Ousmane replied, grinning.

The coaches smiled too. 'Seriously, we've got to lock the doors now. Don't worry, though. You'll be back here tomorrow night for practice.'

At the end of every season, the academy head coaches met with Ousmane and Fatimata for a player evaluation session. It was a chance to look back on the past year and look ahead to next season.

'We want to give you every opportunity, Ousmane,' the head coach for his age group explained after his third year in the academy. 'If you keep playing like this, even more doors are going to open up. You've dominated the Under 15s, so we're already thinking about what's next. Our philosophy is: if you're the best player in the league at your age group, you need to move up to an older age group. That means we'll keep pushing you onto the next level, even if that sounds a little scary.'

Ousmane grinned. That didn't sound scary. It sounded amazing!

The coaches also had some great advice on areas for improvement, and Ousmane listened carefully so he could build those things into his summer workouts. He needed to get a bit stronger, improve his heading and work on his tackling. Another suggestion was increasing his stamina, so he could run for longer stretches, rather than just shorter bursts.

Ousmane nodded. It all made sense.

The head coach smiled, sensing that Ousmane was already thinking about how he could practise those things. Some kids might slump their shoulders when they got feedback about areas to work on, or simply ignore what they were hearing, but the special players embraced it.

After Ousmane and Fatimata left the room, the head coach smiled again.

'That boy is going all the way to the top,' he said to himself. 'I'm sure of it.'

CHAPTER 9

MIKAËL'S BIG PREDICTION

Ousmane was on the fast track through the youth teams. No matter which age group he was playing for, he was still scoring goals and making life miserable for defenders.

Not long after his seventeenth birthday, he was thriving in the Rennes reserves squad too. That also gave him a better chance to measure his progress compared to the first-team players and keep an eye on their results. He just hoped the top coaches were keeping an eye on *him* too!

'Remember, one step at a time,' Fatimata reminded him. 'Put in the hard work and try to get a little better every day. If you do that, good things will happen.'

Ousmane knew his mum was right, but patience

wasn't always his best quality. He would have to keep working on that.

He had definitely improved in his physicality and relentlessness in his years at Rennes, though. He would still get knocked off the ball sometimes, but he never backed down, and he had already chipped in with his first goal and first assist with the reserves. Still, nothing came close to his performance against Hérouville.

It was sparked by an early tackle, with the Hérouville full-back sliding in and clipping Ousmane's ankle. It was a bad foul, and the full-back didn't even apologise. Ousmane was fired up now, and he ripped through the Hérouville defence with an unstoppable hat-trick, and even had time to set up another goal in a huge win.

'The next time we play them, they're going to have to re-think the strategy of fouling you!' Ousmane's teammate David told him as they walked off the pitch together. 'That totally backfired on them today!'

Ousmane laughed. 'I had to make them pay!' he replied, trying to sound like a villain in a film.

The next day, he got a message from Moustapha asking about the game.

He wrote back: 'A 6–1 win, a hat-trick for me and hopefully a promotion to the first team soon!'

But Rennes had other ideas about Ousmane. The first-team coaches chose to keep him in the reserves for a few more games. Ousmane didn't understand. Didn't they think he was ready? What else could he do to prove that he was?

When Mikaël Silvestre arrived as Rennes' new director of football, Ousmane knew he needed a meeting about his future. He had spent most of the summer break battling frustration and confusion. He wanted answers.

'You're an incredible talent,' Mikaël explained. 'It's our job at Rennes to manage the pressure on your shoulders. You're still so young, and your body is still growing. We're going to get you more involved, but we need to do it at the right pace.'

Ousmane trusted Mikaël's opinion. He had played for Sir Alex Ferguson at Manchester United for nine years, alongside some of the all-time greats, like Wayne Rooney, Cristiano Ronaldo and Rio Ferdinand.

After more tense conversations, Ousmane finally got his wish. He would be joining the first team for the 2015–16 season, and he was ready to make a big splash. Some of his new teammates looked like they were almost twice his age – maybe some of them were – but it wasn't long before they understood why Ousmane was there.

Coming off the bench for his debut, he was nervous – but he didn't hide. He called for the ball and tried to take players on. Two weeks later, he had even more to celebrate.

After a sweeping Rennes attack, Ousmane was in the right place at the right time to poke a cross into the net at the back post.

Goooooooooooooooooooooaaaaaaaaaaaaaaaaaa aaaaaaalllllllllllllllllllllllllllll!

His teammates lifted him into the air to celebrate his first goal for the Rennes first team.

'I didn't know if you were going to reach that!' shouted striker Giovanni Sio.

'Thank goodness for your long legs!' added midfielder Gelson Fernandes, laughing.

That goal, together with his success running at defenders, gave Ousmane confidence to keep playing his own unique style, and he could feel himself getting more comfortable with each game.

After one morning practice, Ousmane was taking off his boots and socks when Mikaël walked past, grinning like he was keeping a funny secret from Ousmane.

'What was that all about?' he wondered to himself.

The secret didn't last long. When Ousmane turned on the radio in his car, he understood what Mikaël's grin was all about.

Earlier in the day, Mikaël had spoken to reporters and his quotes were going viral.

Ousmane heard Mikaël's voice coming through his car speakers. *'Ousmane can win the Ballon d'Or. I saw Cristiano Ronaldo at the same age at Manchester United, and Ousmane has the characteristics that remind me of a young Cristiano.'*

Well, that was amazing to hear! Ousmane couldn't

believe it. Rennes clearly saw him as a future star, and he stored those words away for the future – like, for when he had a bad game or lost some of his usual confidence.

It also made him determined to live up to Mikaël's prediction. Maybe for the first time, Ousmane truly believed he could get to the very top of the football world.

CHAPTER 10

TWO-FOOTED MAGIC

The Rennes fans had a new favourite player. Ousmane might not always have a great game, but he usually brought the entertainment – and the home crowd was loudest when he was sprinting up the wing.

Ousmane was loving life in the first team, and the local derby against Nantes was the next big match circled on the calendar. He couldn't wait to see the excitement for that game, but everyone seemed quieter than usual in the dressing room.

'How are you feeling?' one of the coaches asked, probably expecting Ousmane to be nervous.

'I'm too young to feel that pressure!' he answered, grinning and hoping to get a few laughs.

Ousmane felt an extra boost of energy as soon as he

stepped on the pitch. Some days, it was like that – he just sensed that he was going to cause chaos for defenders, and he proved it with an incredible first half.

Rennes started on the attack, and Ousmane lurked on the edge of the box for an early free kick. A Nantes defender cleared the danger with a brave header – or at least, he thought he had. The ball looped towards Ousmane and he reacted fastest. He flung his foot at the ball and steered it through the crowd. Almost in slow motion, it sailed into the top corner.

Gooooooooooooooooooooooaaaaaaaaaaaaaaaaaaa aaaaaaallllllllllllllllllllllllllll!

'You couldn't have placed that any better!' Gelson called, chasing Ousmane over to the touchline to celebrate.

Ousmane's confidence was skyrocketing now. He dropped deep, called for the ball and dipped his shoulder to shake off his marker. In a flash, he raced through the Nantes midfield and fired a shot just wide.

Ousmane grinned as he saw the Nantes defenders pointing at each other and arguing about why he had been left in so much space.

A few minutes later, Rennes won another free kick, and Ousmane grabbed the ball to take it this time. It wasn't the right angle for a shot, so he targeted the crowd of red shirts in the box. He curled a cross into the box, swinging it towards the keeper. Giovanni went for it but couldn't reach it. Two Nantes defenders stretched but couldn't reach it either, and all that movement made the keeper freeze on his line. The ball kept going untouched and ended up in the net.

Goooooooooooooooooooooooaaaaaaaaaaaaaaaaaaa aaaaaaalllllllllllllllllllllllllllll!

This time, Ousmane was in disbelief. That wasn't even a shot. 'Some days, you get the luck!' he told Giovanni as they jogged back to the centre circle.

Now he was drifting all over the pitch, dragging Nantes players out of position and gliding past tackles. On another counterattack, Giovanni whipped a pass into space and Ousmane raced after it. There was just one Nantes defender, their slowest centre-back, between him and the goal.

Ousmane didn't hesitate. He dribbled into the box, opening up the angle for a left-footed shot, tempting the defender into lunging for a block, then shifting the ball onto his right foot instead. He fired a shot into the bottom corner.

Goooooooooooooooooooooooaaaaaaaaaaaaaaaaaaa aaaaaaalllllllllllllllllllllllllllll!

A first-half hat-trick.

'You're making it look easy!' Giovanni yelled, while the home fans made even more noise.

Rennes cruised through the second half, and soon Ousmane was soaking up the applause while the players did a lap of the pitch at the final whistle. The fans saved the biggest cheer for him as he carried the match ball under his arm.

Suddenly, he got a tap on the shoulder. A TV reporter wanted to ask him a few questions.

'Ousmane, you were brilliant today,' the reporter said. 'Is that what we can expect every week now?'

'I hope so!' Ousmane said. 'We really wanted to put on a show today, and it couldn't have gone any better for us.'

'You scored three goals with your right foot, so are you right-footed or left-footed?' the reporter asked.

Ousmane hadn't been expecting that kind of question. He hesitated for a second. 'Erm, left-footed,' he mumbled.

'Don't you take penalties with your right foot?' the interviewer asked.

'Yes.'

'Why?'

'Because I shoot better with my right foot,' Ousmane said.

As he replayed the conversation in his head, he realised he may even have confused himself with those answers.

Of course, when his Rennes teammates heard about the video, they rushed to find it online, and the jokes quickly followed.

'Ousmane, are you right-handed?' one teammate asked.

'But doesn't he sign autographs with his left hand?' added another, and the whole dressing room giggled.

Ousmane laughed too. It probably hadn't been his best interview, but all the banter couldn't spoil his special day.

CHAPTER 11

THE DORTMUND DEAL AND THE PERFECT MENTOR

'In one season, you've gone from ALM Évreux winger to one of Europe's top youngsters,' Moustapha said during one of his visits to 'La Madeleine'. 'I always believed in you, Dembouz!'

Ousmane was happy with Year 1 in the first team at Rennes, but he knew he still wasn't close to unlocking all the levels of his game. That would take plenty more seasons and a lot more matches. But he had proved to the doubters that he was a good fit in France's top division.

In fact, Ousmane had proved that so convincingly that even bigger clubs around Europe wanted to sign him. He wasn't sure if all the reports were true, but he had started to hear the rumours.

'This doesn't happen very often, Ousmane,' his agent explained. 'Your career has taken off faster than anyone could have predicted, and none of the top teams want to miss out on the next young star.'

Suddenly, the phones wouldn't stop ringing at Rennes. Almost every call was about Ousmane.

Manchester United, Liverpool, Bayern Munich and Barcelona were all being linked with him. Those famous clubs were the obvious choices for a transfer, but Ousmane loved the sound of Borussia Dortmund, a German club with an excellent record of developing young players and putting them on the path to big things.

That's when the difficult conversations began, and Ousmane was happy to leave those for his agent. He focused on his summer workouts and checked in for updates whenever he could.

In some ways, he was still in shock. He had only played one season for Rennes. How could all these clubs be so sure that he was going to be a superstar? Were they really ready to spend big money on him?

But he also didn't want to walk away from this opportunity. He spoke to his mum, his friends and other people he trusted in the football world. They all reminded him to do whatever made him happy.

'I want to go to Dortmund,' he told Rennes. 'That's the right move for me.'

Ousmane had always been ambitious with his football career, and he just hoped the Rennes fans would understand his decision. After long conversations, the transfer was finally confirmed, and Ousmane quickly packed a few suitcases for the flight to Germany.

When Ousmane arrived in Dortmund and made his way to the hotel, the nerves sprung up in his stomach. The street signs were in German. The shop signs were in German. The radio was playing in German.

If he hadn't realised before, he knew now that this move to Dortmund was a big change, with a new language, a new country and a new everything.

Dortmund were ready to celebrate when Ousmane arrived. They knew what they were getting – a dynamic youngster who could play in lots of different positions – and the fans were soon rushing to the team shop to buy their Dembélé shirts.

'I can't wait to play in the Bundesliga in front of eighty thousand at the Westfalenstadion and play in the Champions League with my new teammates,' Ousmane told reporters.

He was still thinking about all the recent changes in his life when he walked into the dressing room at the club's training ground. As he opened the door, he almost collided with one of his new teammates.

'Oh, erm, sorry!' he mumbled. When he looked up, he froze.

It was Pierre-Emerick Aubameyang, Dortmund's star striker. He was just as surprised that Pierre-Emerick recognised him.

'Welcome, Ousmane!' he said, shaking hands. 'Call me Auba.'

Ousmane grinned. It was a relief to see another player who had taken his early steps in the French league and made a similar move to Germany.

'I remember what it was like for me when I first got here,' Auba said, putting an arm round Ousmane.

'People don't fully understand it unless they've lived it themselves.'

'What's it like at Dortmund?' Ousmane asked. 'Are you happy here so far?'

'It's a great club with great people who really care,' Auba replied. 'The fans are amazing too. Wait until you see the stadium on matchday! The coaches make sure we work really hard, and that's led to some good results on the pitch.'

Auba signalled for Ousmane to follow him to the club cafeteria, where they picked up water and fruit. 'I'm here to help you settle in, so just ask me if you need anything. I'll introduce you to the rest of the squad before training starts.'

It took Ousmane about fifteen minutes of his first training session to see that Auba wasn't joking about the hard work.

'Is it always like this?' he asked, crouching over and breathing heavily.

'I tried to warn you!' Auba said, laughing. 'Come on, you're supposed to be the young guy!'

Ousmane grinned, but he was beginning to

understand the Dortmund standards.

'I'll do whatever it takes to succeed here,' he told his mum that night. 'You can see why Dortmund have been so successful. The coaches think of every little detail, and it's just right for a young player.'

Ousmane's legs were still burning from the day's sprints, but he didn't care. He was too busy thinking about what it would be like to play on the wing, teaming up with Auba and winger Marco Reus. Ousmane bounced out of bed the next morning, ready for more.

The next week, Ousmane and Auba met up for dinner. 'We can try some real German food,' Auba had suggested, but Ousmane was struggling to read the menu.

'Don't worry, I'll order for you,' Auba said, sensing Ousmane's uncertainty. Then he grinned. 'Remind me, what are your least favourite foods? I'll make sure you get double helpings of those.'

'Don't you dare!' Ousmane said, laughing.

He quickly formed a great connection with manager Thomas Tuchel too. Like Ousmane, Coach Tuchel was young, ambitious and hungry to win trophies. The clock was always ticking for Dortmund as they tried to keep hold of their best players, so the 2016–17 season would be another important one.

When Ousmane signed autographs after training, he saw yellow and black everywhere. The fans were so passionate, and the atmosphere was even better in the stadium, with Dortmund's loudest supporters behind the goal in a section called The Wall.

'When we're tired or we're losing, the fans give us such a boost,' Ousmane told his friends after the first preseason friendly. 'They never stop singing.'

One of those friends had already followed Ousmane to Dortmund. Moustapha signed a deal with the club's reserve team, and they were soon reunited as roommates. That made it even easier for Ousmane to feel at home in his new city.

In training, he made a strong start. With Coach Tuchel encouraging him to roam from one wing to the other, Ousmane felt the freedom to play his best football. But he still looked over at his manager nervously after losing the ball on one counterattack.

He expected to see Coach Tuchel shaking his head in frustration, but it was the opposite. He was clapping Ousmane for being brave enough to try something creative.

'I always want you to express yourself out there,' Coach Tuchel told him after training. 'You've got everything you need to become a great player, and we're going to get there together.'

Ousmane felt ten feet tall as he made the short journey back to his hotel.

CHAPTER 12

FRANCE'S TOP YOUNG TALENT

What?!! Ousmane's head was spinning. A call-up to the France squad? Was this a prank? He had already played for the French youth teams, but this was a whole different conversation.

'Ousmane, are you still there?' the voice on the phone asked patiently. It was Didier Deschamps, the France manager.

It must be real, Ousmane decided. 'Yes, sorry, I'm here,' he replied, finally. 'I'm just in shock, to be honest.'

He knew he had been playing well, but there were so many good French wingers. Even after some injuries in the squad, Ousmane wasn't expecting this phone call.

Coach Deschamps didn't have any doubts, though. He understood Ousmane's qualities – his speed, his ability to play on either wing, his direct style – and he wanted to see how they translated to international football.

'We've been watching you since your Rennes days,' Coach Deschamps continued. 'The upcoming games against Italy and Belarus are the perfect time to bring you into the camp, and we're looking forward to working with you.'

The shock gradually wore off, but the excitement didn't. Ousmane called his family and friends to spread the news, and he was soon travelling to meet up with the rest of the squad. He was about to come face-to-face with the French legends he had watched on TV at previous World Cups and European Championships. He quickly prepared a few things to say in case he was too overwhelmed when he met them.

With a fancy hotel and a beautiful training kit, this felt like the top of the football world. Ousmane didn't have long to think about that, though.

He could feel his body shaking a little as he met

Antoine Griezmann, Olivier Giroud, Hugo Lloris and the rest of the squad.

At the end of the first session, Ousmane ended up on a five-a-side team with Antoine and Olivier. He tried not to look too starstruck, and he didn't want to let them down, even in a game that meant nothing.

After training, a room full of reporters wanted to speak to him, and the questions came fast:

How are you settling into the squad?
What's surprised you the most so far?
Is it what you pictured so far?
Do you expect to play in the two games this week?

Ousmane did his best to answer them without saying something silly or giving away any information that was meant to stay private. It was just as nerve-racking as sharing a training pitch with his new France teammates.

By the time he got back to his room, he was so exhausted that he fell asleep instantly. But he felt refreshed again the next day, and he didn't hold back during the one-on-one drills against the best French defenders. He must have done something right because Coach Deschamps told him to stay ready as one of the options off the bench against Italy to bring pace and energy in the second half.

Ousmane stood with the other substitutes for the national anthem as a mix of emotions swept over him. At least he had some time to get over that before he came on – *if* he came on.

With thirty minutes to go, Coach Deschamps signalled to the group of subs warming up near the dugout, and one of the coaches hurried towards Ousmane.

Ousmane's first reaction was 'Me?!' But luckily, he recovered quickly and took off his warm-up top. There was no time to think about anything now. His debut for France was just seconds away! He just took a deep breath and listened to the final instructions on where he would be playing.

'You're going on for Antoine,' the coach explained. 'You can tuck inside when we're attacking, but make sure you get back when we're defending.'

As Antoine jogged off, he stopped to give Ousmane a high-five.

'Congrats, Ousmane,' Antoine told him. 'One rule – make sure you enjoy it!'

Ousmane looked down at his chest and saw the cockerel on the famous France shirt. He was relieved to get a few early touches to settle his nerves, and he was on the pitch for the third French goal in a 3–1 win. For some players, it may have felt like a meaningless friendly, but that night would always mean something special to Ousmane.

He got another chance in the 0–0 draw with Belarus a few days later. France didn't play their best football, but Ousmane still felt the thrill of representing his country again. A few months later, he scored his first international goal against England, firing home the winner in a 3–2 victory.

Most conversations about France's potential started with Kylian Mbappé, the team's other teenage sensation. With Ousmane ready to shine alongside him, the future was bright.

CHAPTER 13

UP FOR THE CUP

'We're ninety minutes away from the final,' Coach Tuchel said, standing in the middle of the dressing room and giving his final instructions before Dortmund's German Cup semifinal against Bayern Munich. 'We love being the underdogs. Guess what? Tonight, we're the underdogs.'

Bayern Munich were the giants of the German league, with Robert Lewandowski, Arjen Robben, Franck Ribéry and Xabi Alonso. Ousmane respected them, but there was no fear, not even when they were losing 2–1 in the second half.

'We're still in this game!' he shouted, glancing up at the clock on the scoreboard. Coach Tuchel had pushed his players to be ready for a big finish. Bayern had some older players, so there could be tired legs late in the match.

Ousmane dropped a little deeper to get involved, and he saw that the Bayern defenders didn't want to follow him, in case he suddenly spun behind them.

He laid the ball off and kept running. As the return pass fizzed through to him, he glided into the penalty area, but there were still five red Bayern shirts in his way and just Auba to aim for.

It was worth a try, Ousmane thought. He floated a cross over the heads of everyone. Well, everyone except Auba, who jumped to head the ball in at the back post.

Yes!! Auba ran over to Ousmane, pointing and grinning. 'What a cross, buddy!' he shouted. 'I can't believe you got that to me!'

The Bayern crowd was stunned – and Ousmane wasn't done yet. Marco won the ball in midfield and suddenly the counterattack was on. Ousmane rushed forward to support him.

At first, Ousmane was disappointed that Marco played the pass to the left, instead of to him on the right. But then the ball found its way back across the box. This time, Marco spotted Ousmane and set him up with a tight angle.

Ousmane still only had one thought in his mind: make space for a shot.

The Bayern full-back charged across, but he was out of control. Ousmane faked the shot and shifted the ball onto his left foot instead. Before anyone else could get near him, he took his chance. He didn't try to hit it too hard – a power shot might have sent the ball sailing into the crowd. Instead, he gave it just enough curl and dip. The ball clipped the underside of the bar and bounced into the net. *3–2!*

Gooooooooooooooooooooooaaaaaaaaaaaaaaaaaaa aaaaaaalllllllllllllllllllllllllllll!

Ousmane had a million ideas flying through his head for a goal celebration, but in the end, he just ran across the pitch and slid on his knees in front of the Dortmund bench. The subs, the coaches and even Coach Tuchel were there to congratulate him.

Now they had to stay calm. Ousmane tracked back desperately, closing down space and letting the seconds tick away. At last, the referee blew the final whistle, and the Dortmund players could celebrate. Most of them were too tired to do more than lift their arms into the air, but they limped their way into a little huddle. It was one of the sweetest wins of Ousmane's life.

'We never give up!' Auba said, hugging Ousmane. 'And what a winning goal, buddy. Left foot. Top corner. Bang!'

'I guess watching you in shooting practice paid off!' Ousmane replied.

Coach Tuchel jogged onto the pitch to join his players. 'Ousmane, that was magic!' he said, wrapping him in a hug.

But then it was back to business. There were league games still on the calendar and a cup final against Eintracht Frankfurt to think about. Ousmane counted down the days to the final. This was a chance to win a trophy in his first season with Dortmund and give the fans a big party to kick off the summer.

'Nervous?' Auba asked as they sat together on the team bus on the way to the final.

'Kind of nervous, kind of excited,' Ousmane answered.

This was the fourth straight year that Dortmund had reached the final, and the players hadn't forgotten the pain of losing last season's final on penalties.

'That one really hurt,' Auba admitted. 'It's such a horrible way to lose.'

'Well, let's make sure it doesn't get to penalties this time!' Ousmane added, grinning.

During the warm-up, Ousmane looked up to see Coach Tuchel walking along the touchline towards him.

'Make your mark on the game,' said Coach Tuchel. 'Don't wait for things to happen. Make them happen yourself.'

'I'm ready!' Ousmane replied. 'We're bringing the trophy home tonight, boss.'

Ousmane lived up to his promise by racing forward to support an early attack. When the ball bounced his way, he escaped his marker and didn't hesitate, whipping a quick shot around another defender and past the keeper's dive.

Gooooooooooooooooooooooaaaaaaaaaaaaaaaaaaa aaaaaaalllllllllllllllllllllllllllll!

What a start – 1–0! Ousmane had dreamed of scoring a cup final goal ever since he was a little boy playing at 'La Madeleine'. Now he had actually done it.

Dortmund battled their way to a 2–1 win, and everything after that felt like madness. There was singing, there was music pumping, and some of the players were using kit containers as drums. At the same moment, the trophy was being passed around and waved from side to side. Ousmane knew that the party would be rocking back in Dortmund too.

But some of that joy slipped away when Ousmane heard that Dortmund would be saying goodbye to Coach Tuchel, and he wanted some answers on what had happened. Coach Tuchel had got the best out of him all season, and he was a big reason that Ousmane had won the Young Player of the Year award.

What did this mean for Ousmane's own future at the club? He had a bad feeling about all of it, and he carried that disappointment into a summer of more twists and turns.

CHAPTER 14

BARCA AT ALL COSTS

Just when Ousmane thought the surprises were over and life might slow down a little, another big decision landed at his feet.

'Barcelona are interested in you and they're going to make an offer,' his agent told him. 'Here's a sentence you probably never expected to hear: Barca want to sign you to replace Neymar.'

Ousmane laughed. He didn't know how else to react. He already knew that Neymar had just signed with PSG. But Barcelona still had Lionel Messi, Andrés Iniesta and Luis Suárez. They weren't exactly short of star attackers.

'So, do we just wait and see what happens?' asked Ousmane.

But even as he said the words, he knew that would be impossible. This was Barcelona, one of the biggest clubs in the world. Even in the seconds since he had heard the news, his world had stopped – or at least that's how it felt. He needed to find out more. Who wouldn't want to play for a huge club like Barcelona?

Sure, he could wait a few years, but maybe this opportunity wouldn't be there again. How could he walk away from this golden ticket?

Equally, Dortmund saw Ousmane as a big part of their future. The message was understandable – they had only signed him a year ago and he would probably be even better next season.

When the transfer discussions hit a brick wall, Ousmane's frustration grew. What options did he have?

If Dortmund weren't going to do what he wanted, Ousmane decided he would have to take his own steps. He didn't feel good about it, but he stopped going to training with his teammates in protest. He would later think about other ways he could have handled the situation, ways that would have led to fewer headlines and less criticism. In that moment, though, he was desperate for his dream move.

There were plenty of hurt feelings at Dortmund, but they eventually agreed a deal with Barcelona. Ousmane became the joint second-most-expensive football player in the world, as reports put the transfer fee at €105 million.

Ousmane tried to put the past few months out of his mind when he arrived at Camp Nou for a special press conference to officially announce his signing. He had watched enough of these events to know what was expected, and he brought out his biggest smile. One of the staff hurried into the room and passed him a Barcelona shirt. Ousmane turned it around and saw his name on the back.

'Look this way, Ousmane!' the photographer called. 'Now hold up the shirt.'

With a ball at his feet, he went through a few flicks and keepy-ups, then took a closer look at the famous stadium. The big price tag meant big pressure on Ousmane's shoulders, but the good news was that he was joining an unbelievable team, and it wasn't like he would have do it all alone.

'It's always been my dream to be at Barcelona and now I'm here I'm very happy,' Ousmane explained to the media. 'It is the best club in the world with the best players in the world.'

The preseason was a blur, from sweating his way through practice sessions to moving into a nice house in the city. Ousmane felt like a little kid on his first day of training. It reminded him of the first day at a new school, except this time he would be meeting Messi, Iniesta and Luis Suárez. That made it a little different!

'Welcome to Barca, Ousmane!' Leo said, high-fiving him. That instantly became the highlight of Ousmane's Barcelona tour.

'Now I can tell my friends that Lionel Messi knows who I am!' Ousmane replied, laughing. 'I'm so excited to be your teammate!'

'Well, we're going to really need you this year,' Leo added. 'We've got to make up for last season and win the league trophy back.'

Ousmane nodded. He loved watching all the European leagues, so he knew that Real Madrid had won the Spanish league last season, finishing just three points ahead of Barcelona. He had heard many stories about El Clásico games between the two legendary clubs, and he couldn't wait to experience it for himself.

The buzz was building, but Ousmane's fast rise was about to hit some bumps.

CHAPTER 15

INJURY SETBACKS

There was always an adjustment period for new players as they learned the Barcelona style of play. The coaches pushed Ousmane hard in training, helping him understand the team's passing patterns and how he would fit into their formation. They also explained that they would ease him into his first season in Spain. That all sounded good, but Ousmane was itching to play.

He started on the bench in the first game of the season at home to Espanyol, and that gave him a first chance to soak in the Camp Nou experience, with the stadium crammed full of fans almost up to the sky. He would have loved to be starting, but at least he could get used to the atmosphere.

In the second half, Coach Valverde called for Ousmane to warm up. Three minutes later, Ousmane was standing on the touchline, about to make his Barcelona debut. The home fans clapped and cheered as their new signing ran onto the pitch, and they were even happier when he set up Luis to make it 5–0.

'If you keep doing that, the fans are going to love you!' Luis said, giving Ousmane a high-five.

That highlight moment earned Ousmane a place in the starting lineup against Getafe a week later, and he almost danced out of the room when he got that news.

But that joy was soon replaced with tears. Chasing the ball near the corner flag, Ousmane cut inside and tried to hold off his marker. As he stretched, he felt a sharp pain in his leg. When the ball went out for a goal kick, he tried to jog back into position on the wing, but he couldn't move properly. He stopped and sat down on the turf, signalling for treatment.

His teammates came over to check on him, and he pointed to where he had felt the pain, while shaking his head and fighting back tears. He knew he would have to come off.

Ousmane walked slowly off the pitch with the Barcelona physio. It was too soon for Ousmane to know if it was a serious injury, but he already felt the emotions swirling through his head – the disappointment, anger, sadness. He had felt good in training all week. Why did this have to happen now?

After a quick conversation with the physio and the Barcelona doctor, Ousmane just sat in the dressing room with a towel over his face. He had pictured so many different things for his debut, but this wasn't one of them.

'You'll come back even stronger,' Andrés explained, trying to reassure him. 'We've all been through this kind of setback in our careers and we're here to support you.'

'Thanks, Andrés,' he managed to reply, but he wasn't really ready to talk about it yet.

The next day, Ousmane was booked in for treatment and further tests to see how badly the muscle was injured. The news grew worse. It was a serious muscle tear, and it would take at least three months before Ousmane could get back on the pitch.

'Three months?!' he asked, slumping down in his chair. 'But it doesn't feel too bad today.'

'The results show some real damage there, and you could make the injury even worse if you're not resting it,' the doctor replied. 'Sadly, these things don't just heal overnight.'

Ousmane sighed. This would mean a new reality, with lots of rest and eventually exercises to do every morning and every evening. He filled the hours with video games and TV to take his mind off the boredom.

Whenever he visited the training ground for treatment or check-ups, he could see his teammates training outside. They always tried to cheer him up, but he just wanted to be out there with them. Even when he had made enough progress to move to light gym workouts, Ousmane still knew he was weeks away from practices and the real games.

He had to wait until January to return to the team, but it felt amazing to be back. He had missed every little part of the gameday experience, and he had never been so happy to do a warm-up. But two weeks later, he was back on the treatment table, with a familiar sinking feeling in his stomach – he was going to be missing more games. He and Andrés were both injured, and Ousmane's first season at Barcelona was slipping away. He had barely kicked a ball yet.

'Ousmane, you've got years ahead of you at Barcelona when you're back,' Fatimata told him when she called to get the injury update.

'I know, but I want to show everyone what I can do,' he answered in a sad voice. 'My teammates, my coaches, the fans – none of them have seen the real Ousmane yet.'

As he became stronger and stronger, Ousmane started looking at the fixture list to target a return date. The doctors cleared him for training, and the coaches urged him to take it slowly. But how was he supposed to do that? He needed to go at 100 per cent to keep up with his teammates.

Ousmane was back in the European spotlight for the Champions League quarter-final second leg against Chelsea, and he was determined to make up for lost time. When Leo broke free on the left,

Ousmane sprinted to support him, and Luis made a run in the box.

Leo used Luis as a decoy, fooling the Chelsea defenders into following that run. Instead, he disguised a pass right onto Ousmane's foot. Ousmane took a touch to steady himself, then thundered a shot towards the net, taking out the frustration of his difficult year. The ball flew past the keeper, past the defender on the line and into the top corner.

Goooooooooooooooooooooooaaaaaaaaaaaaaaaaaaa aaaaaaalllllllllllllllllllllllllllll!

Hurray, his first goal for Barcelona! The Camp Nou erupted into a loud cheer, and Ousmane pointed back at Leo, thanking him for the perfect pass. Leo knew what it meant to him, and he jumped into Ousmane's arms. Finally, their partnership was up and running.

Barcelona took a cautious approach, subbing Ousmane off in the second half, but he grinned as he headed for the bench and took a few extra seconds to enjoy the fans' applause. This was the kind of night he had pictured when he moved to Barca.

Barcelona went on to win the Spanish league and cup double that year, 2018, and, as he looked at the medals, Ousmane was happy to put the injuries behind him and focus on the future.

'I'm already counting the days until next season,' he told Moustapha, who had moved to join him in Barcelona. 'There's no stopping us now!'

CHAPTER 16

WARNING SIGNS

The fame was something new for Ousmane. Sure, he had been recognised in the street when he played for Nantes and Dortmund, but this was another level of attention. He loved the passion of the fans on matchdays, but he preferred a quieter life the rest of the time.

That meant more nights at home – and more nights staying up late to play video games.

'Have you made any new friends?' Fatimata asked him when she came to visit.

'Do the players on the NBA2K game count?' Ousmane joked. 'I've been spending a lot of time with them lately, and we've built a great connection.'

That wasn't funny for long, though. The late nights

started to become a bigger problem, putting his Barcelona career at risk.

One morning, Ousmane woke up on the sofa next to his video game controller. He reached over to pick up his phone and check the time. Then he froze.

'Oh no!' he shouted, sitting up. 'I'm going to be so late!'

He was supposed to have been at Barcelona's morning training session an hour earlier. The coaches had already spoken to him about needing to be more professional. Like all his teammates were, he was expected to get himself to training on time.

When he finally got to the training ground, Coach Valverde spotted him and signalled for him to come over. After a short conversation on the touchline, Ousmane was sent to train by himself, away from the rest of the squad.

Ousmane looked at the ground. He had let himself down, but he was determined to prove he could do better. This wasn't his first warning for turning up late, either.

'We expect a lot of Dembélé and we made a big

effort to bring him to Barcelona,' the club explained when they were asked about it. 'We are going to work with him to improve the situation.'

The message was clear: *'If you don't take this more seriously, Barcelona isn't the right club for you.'*

Ousmane knew he had to make some changes in his life. He could see the disappointment on his teammates' faces, and it was even harder to hear the frustration in their voices.

'Look, we get it, you're a young guy in a new city,' Leo said. 'We're going to help you focus on football.'

The Barcelona coaches weren't there to babysit him. Instead, they encouraged him to put the mistakes behind him and find some solutions.

Setting an alarm, or two alarms even.
Keeping his phone on so he could be contacted.
Limiting his video game time at night.

Ousmane wanted to prove that he was taking the feedback seriously. That meant forming new habits that would keep him on track. The next day, his alarm sounded and Ousmane hurried to have breakfast and pack his bag. That morning, he was one of the first players to arrive at training.

The coaches noticed his efforts, and exchanged nods, but they needed to see him doing that consistently. It wasn't enough to just make the effort the day after getting in trouble.

Leo and midfielder Sergio Busquets were good role models to follow, and Ousmane tried to learn from them. He saw the way they looked after their bodies during rest days and how serious they were about the recovery process after games – what they ate, what treatment they had, what exercises they did.

That's what he needed to do, rather than just sitting on his sofa and watching TV or playing video games. It was all part of the learning process for Ousmane – he was still just twenty-one years old. But there could be no more excuses now. He had been warned.

He had to ask himself: *Am I focused enough on my football?*

He worked hard to avoid slipping back into bad habits, and he could see the difference it was making in his training performances. But just as he was starting to feel great about the way the season was going, disaster struck again.

'No! No! No!' Ousmane screamed, slapping the grass in despair and grabbing his leg. 'Not again!'

The Barcelona physio hurried onto the pitch. He did a few exercises with Ousmane and quickly signalled to the bench for a substitution.

Ousmane's career in Spain had already been dominated by injuries, and now he was going to miss more time. This hadn't been an issue during his youth football years. Back then, he was always fit enough to play every match. As he limped off, all he could think about was the long road back – again.

CHAPTER 17

A WORLD CUP ROLLERCOASTER: PART I

That summer, some of Ousmane's friends were preparing for holidays in the sun, but he was off on a different kind of adventure – the 2018 World Cup. The timing was ideal, really. He had finished his injury recovery, and he guessed he was fresher than most players who had been through a full league season.

Though Ousmane was still getting used to the international stage and training alongside so many experienced players, he had shown the France coaches they could trust him.

'You wouldn't be in the squad if we didn't believe in you,' Coach Deschamps told Ousmane as they discussed the tournament. 'We've got to keep pushing the next wave of French stars, and we think you're part of that group.'

More than anything, the World Cup experience put Ousmane in a great mood. He had some fun memories of watching the tournament as a kid. He was still a baby when France stunned Brazil at the 1998 World Cup, but he had cheered the team on in 2006 when they made it all the way to the final, before losing on penalties.

That 2006 team was special, with Zinedine Zidane and Thierry Henry, and the current French squad had plenty of star names too. When Ousmane boarded the plane for the flight to Russia for the tournament, he glanced up the aisle and saw Antoine, Olivier, N'Golo Kanté and Paul Pogba. He sat down next to Kylian Mbappé and started scrolling through the films.

'We were at school when the last World Cup was happening!' Ousmane said, looking over at Kylian. 'It's all kind of mad, isn't it?'

Kylian laughed. He was a year younger than Ousmane and already lighting up the French league. 'You're right, it really is!' he said. 'Sometimes

I'm scared that I'll wake up and find out it was just a dream!'

But this wasn't going to be a holiday. That was clear from the very first training session, after which Ousmane had to lie down on the bed when he got back to his hotel room. Coach Deschamps wanted all the players to be ready for the first group game against Australia, and Ousmane knew that every practice was another chance to show what he could do.

When the starting lineup was announced, he was stunned to hear his name. Coach Deschamps was putting a lot of trust in Ousmane, especially when expectations were so high for France at this tournament.

At one of the team dinners, Olivier joined Ousmane's table and pulled over a spare chair.

'How are you feeling, hotshot?' he asked.

'Definitely a little nervous,' Ousmane admitted. 'Any tips?'

'It's normal to have those nerves,' Olivier replied. 'It sounds like an easy thing to say, but try to enjoy it. This is the World Cup, and I'm sure you dreamed of this moment when you were a little kid.'

'I did!' Ousmane answered. 'That feels like just a few years ago really!'

Olivier laughed. 'Well, one day, you'll be the one sitting on this side of the table talking to young teammates,' he said. 'But until then, go out and have fun. Listen, learn and take every chance to improve.'

The older players set the example, but the youngsters brought the energy and the laughs. In other squads, Ousmane might have felt uncomfortable as such a young player. But the France dressing room had plenty, led by Kylian.

At last, it was time for the action to start. Lining up for the anthems, Ousmane could feel the emotions kicking in. He was nervous, happy, proud and excited, all at once. He just hoped he would still remember how to dribble the ball.

But Australia made life difficult. Ousmane was tightly marked, and he couldn't link up with Kylian and Antoine. It just wasn't his day. He was subbed off in the second half and watched from the bench while France scored a late winner.

There were lots of relieved faces in the dressing

room afterwards, and Ousmane tried to take it all in. Even though he wished he had made a bigger impact, how could he be disappointed? He reminded himself that he was playing at *the World Cup*. When he left the stadium and walked out to the team bus, he saw a crowd of French fans who had stayed behind in the hope of seeing their heroes and getting some autographs.

'Ousmane! Ousmane!' one boy called, holding up his France shirt.

Ousmane checked to make sure the bus wasn't going to leave without him, then hurried over to sign the shirt.

'You're my favourite player!' the boy said, with a huge smile on his face.

'Thanks for the support!' Ousmane said, smiling back. 'We'll be better in the next game!'

Back at the hotel, he replayed some moments from the match in his head, thinking about what he could have done differently. He wasn't sure, so he found it helpful to watch a few video clips with the coaches. They talked about runs he could have made and times where he could have stayed wider on the wing or been a bit more patient with the ball.

With the group games spaced out and lots of time off in between, Ousmane got to know his teammates much better, and he called home regularly to speak to his family and friends.

Ousmane also loved watching the World Cup action from other groups. There were no bad games! Some of his teammates preferred to use their free time in other ways, but he needed to catch up on the latest scores. Lots of his Barcelona teammates were there for the tournament too, and Ousmane was in the middle of all the banter in the group chat. Which of them would come back with the bragging rights?

Ousmane dropped to the bench for the next game, but he got another chance in the final group match against Denmark. This time, he was sharper, and he found enough space to get oohs and aahs from the crowd as he dribbled past defenders.

France made it through to the knockout rounds, and Coach Deschamps spoke to Ousmane at the end of one training session. 'You've done a great job, Ousmane,' he said. 'You're growing as a player every time you step onto the pitch, and that's so exciting for the years ahead. I'm going to rely a bit more on the senior players in these knockout games – but stay ready.'

Ousmane understood. The pressure went up another level in the knockout games. They were always one bad game away from packing their bags, and there were other attackers with a lot more experience. Ousmane just focused on being a good teammate, and he had a front row seat for the dramatic win over Argentina in the next round.

Ousmane would have loved to be a bigger part of the action, but he was happy to see the team winning. He also remembered what Olivier had told him – all of these experiences would be valuable for the rest of his career.

France reached the World Cup final, and millions of people around the world would be watching them battle Croatia. Ousmane was a substitute again, but he felt the butterflies in his stomach when the game kicked off. He wondered how his teammates were managing the nerves on the pitch.

When France took over in the second half, Ousmane could relax a little, and he ran over to celebrate near the corner flag when Paul Pogba scored their fourth goal. As he sat down again, a thought popped into his head – he was about to get an up-close view of the famous World Cup trophy!

Ousmane walked up proudly to get his medal, and he could see France flags everywhere as he shook hands with the line of people on the stage.

'We're going home as heroes!' Kylian said, putting his arm round Ousmane while they posed for photos.

When it was Ousmane's turn to hold the trophy, he could hardly believe this was actually happening. He was terrified about dropping it – or even worse, breaking it.

The party went on late into the night, and Ousmane knew the World Cup memories would last much longer. This was just the start of Ousmane's international career, but he had experienced so much in such a short amount of time. He couldn't wait to see what was next.

CHAPTER 18

LAUGHS WITH LEO

Back in Barcelona, Ousmane was still feeling the World Cup glow. That definitely made up for a shortened summer break. But there were new tests ahead in the 2018–19 season and, as always, there were big expectations at Barca.

But that didn't mean the players couldn't still have some fun. Ousmane made sure there were lots of laughs, and Lionel Messi was often part of them.

'Leo, look at this!' Ousmane called one morning when he arrived for training. He held up a photo on his phone.

Leo jogged over and took the phone. He burst into laughter.

The photo was Ousmane in a Barcelona shirt with 'Messi 10' on the back from the early stages of his own football journey. His mum had sent it to him that morning while going through old memories.

'That's amazing!' Leo said. 'We were destined to play together!'

'It's an honour, man,' Ousmane added. 'You're the GOAT!'

'How old are you in that photo?' Leo asked. 'Actually, don't answer that. That'll just make me feel even older.'

'It was probably around the same age that I had your posters and football cards too,' Ousmane teased. 'Everyone needs a childhood hero.'

'Okay, new topic!' Leo said, grinning. 'How many goals are we going to score this season? We got ninety-nine last year, but I think we can get to one hundred this time.'

It was unbelievable to play with Leo. Ousmane imagined that must have been how people felt about playing with Pelé or Maradona too. The opportunities to link up with Leo had been limited with Ousmane's injuries, but their summer practice sessions were making a difference. It had reached the point where whenever Leo turned with the ball, he could find the right angle for getting the ball to Ousmane. Even the Barcelona defenders, who saw the pair every day in training, couldn't stop the connection.

Ousmane was a skilful player. That had always been one of his biggest strengths, but he was still stunned by what Leo could do with the ball – wriggling out of tight spaces, leaving defenders on the ground or hitting a perfect pass. It was like he had four sets of eyes to see everything on the pitch.

When the new season kicked off, Ousmane was ready to go. 'I'm fully fit, I've had a good preseason and now I can finally make a difference for Barca,' he told Leo and Luis as they warmed up in training, all effortlessly flicking the ball around without it touching the ground.

Having announced his return, Ousmane didn't waste any time:

With Barcelona drawing 1–1 in the Spanish Super Cup, he surged forward and unleashed a rocket strike into the top corner.

Gooooooooooooooooooooooaaaaaaaaaaaaaaaaaa aaaaaaallllllllllllllllllllllllllll!

With Barcelona drawing 0–0 away to Real Valladolid, Ousmane reacted fastest to sweep a low shot past the keeper.

Gooooooooooooooooooooooaaaaaaaaaaaaaaaaaaaaaaaaaalllllllllllllllllllllllllll!

With Barcelona drawing 1–1 against Real Sociedad, Ousmane swooped in on a scuffed clearance and whipped a left-footed shot into the net.

Gooooooooooooooooooooooaaaaaaaaaaaaaaaaaaaaaaaaaalllllllllllllllllllllllllll!

'This is more like it!' he told Leo. 'These are the moments I imagined when I got here.'

He kept up his scoring form against Arsenal in the Champions League, making himself even more popular with the Barcelona fans.

'Last season, I'm sure some fans were wondering why Barcelona signed me,' he admitted to Moustapha one night while they played video games. 'But now they're starting to see the real Ousmane.'

'If anyone had asked me, I'd have told them,' Moustapha replied. 'Dembouz is the man! He's a magician! He's a wizard!'

Ousmane laughed. 'I know what you're doing,' he said. 'You're saying nice things about me so that I'll be distracted and let you score.'

'It was worth a try,' Moustapha answered, laughing and pretending to throw his controller on the floor when Ousmane scored again.

There was a good balance in Ousmane's life these days. He could still have fun, but football was the main thing on his mind. He was training harder, eating more healthily and smiling even more often.

Barcelona were reaping the rewards from that too. The race for the Spanish league title was heating up, but Barca were the team to beat, especially when Ousmane was finding his best form.

'There's a long way to go,' he admitted when he spoke to his mum before the latest big game. 'But if we keep playing like this, that trophy is ours.'

CHAPTER 19

A GOAL TO REMEMBER

There was nothing better than Champions League nights, and it was no exception when Barca faced an important game against Tottenham. Ousmane arrived at Camp Nou with an extra jolt of energy, and he felt it all the way through the warm-up.

Despite Ousmane's good start to the season, he still felt he had something to prove to the Barcelona fans. He had won over some of the doubters, but he had to keep raising the bar. That same week, he had heard comments on TV which questioned if he was destined to be a talented player who could never quite reach his potential.

'I'm still only twenty-one years old,' he wanted to scream back at them. 'Don't judge me yet!'

But he had to think one game at a time, starting with tonight's match. As usual, Camp Nou was rocking before kick-off, and it didn't take long for the volume of the crowd to go even louder.

Ousmane dropped back to help defend, but he always had one eye on the counterattack. Barcelona cleared the ball, and it looped towards a Tottenham player. Ousmane didn't give up on it, though. He sprinted to lead the press, and a bad Tottenham touch gave him an unexpected chance.

'Go, Ousmane, go!' yelled Coach Valverde from the touchline. The fans were roaring too, sensing something special.

Ousmane muscled the Tottenham defender off the ball and raced forward. He was still on the halfway line, but he had yards of almost-empty pitch in front of him.

He dribbled on, and the last two defenders backed off. He took his time and knocked the ball past one of them. Out of the corner of his eye, he spotted the other defender rushing over. He faked the shot, let the defender slide past and fired a low shot past the keeper.

Goooooooooooooooooooooooaaaaaaaaaaaaaaaaaaa aaaaaaalllllllllllllllllllllllllll!

Ousmane was already skipping towards the corner flag, tapping his head. That was like one of his solo goals for ALM Évreux.

'A Dembélé golazo!' his teammates shouted.

'I've been waiting for a chance like that!' Ousmane called back. It was hard to hear anything with so many fans cheering.

The game finished 1–1, but Ousmane's goal was the main thing that people wanted to talk about. It was soon named UEFA's Goal of the Week.

Barcelona also kept up their league form, including a 2–0 win over Celta Vigo, thanks to goals from Ousmane and Leo.

'Why do you think this partnership is so successful?' a reporter wanted to know.

'It's this guy,' Ousmane explained, pointing at Leo.

'No, no,' Leo argued, with a grin. 'Ousmane is just making me look good this season.'

Every game mattered at this stage of the season. Coach Valverde made that point to his players over and over again, and Ousmane hadn't forgotten. All the good vibes would disappear in a hurry if Atlético Madrid or Real Madrid closed the gap. But Barca refused to slip up, and Ousmane was soon enjoying another trophy party.

He had won two Spanish league titles since signing for Barcelona, but this second one was so much more special for him than his first injury-hit year. This time, he had scored goals, set up goals and played his part in a great season.

But just as Ousmane was thinking about how he could become even more dangerous on the pitch, his body had other ideas.

CHAPTER 20

NEVER GIVE UP

'Can you stand up?' the Barcelona physio asked.

Ousmane tried to move his leg and immediately winced as he felt a sharp pain. He looked to his right and saw the substitutes warming up. It was the first game of the season, and Ousmane felt like he was reliving a nightmare. It was happening again.

His teammates knew it. One by one, they came over to put a hand on his back.

'You'll bounce back from this,' Leo said, squatting down next to Ousmane.

'Let the physios work their magic,' added Antoine, who had signed for Barca that summer.

In a flash, Ousmane's big plans for the season had been ripped apart. That injury cost him most of the

2019–20 season, one of the strangest years ever due to the COVID-19 health crisis that paused sports leagues all over the world.

Then a knee injury ended his time at the delayed Euro 2020 tournament. He had been one of France's sharpest players in their first game against Hungary after coming on as a sub, creating chances with weaving runs on the wing. Minutes later, he was limping off again.

Ousmane tried to make sense of it all. Was it just bad luck? Was there anything he could do to protect himself better? Was some of this happening because his body was still growing?

The Barcelona doctors and physios worked with him on different treatments and exercises, as well as other little changes he could make in his daily routine.

'I'm willing to try anything,' Ousmane said as he sat in another meeting with a doctor.

He still loved football. That hadn't changed. But it was so hard to sit in the stands week after week. He couldn't help his teammates, and he had no outlet for all his energy.

Ousmane needed support to get through these tough times. There were no simple instructions for how to handle this kind of situation, where he was cut off from football for such a long time. Thankfully, he had lots of people to turn to when he just needed a quick meetup or video call to boost his morale.

'This latest recovery is the worst one so far,' he told his mum. 'It's such a lonely experience.'

'I'm happy you're telling me this,' she said. 'It's important to talk about it. We're going to get through this together, and it'll just be a distant memory when you're back on the pitch scoring goals for Barcelona and France.'

Little by little, Ousmane's attitude changed. Instead of feeling sorry for himself, he saw it as an opportunity to show that nothing could break him. He was going to come back better than ever.

But he knew that Barcelona couldn't wait forever for him to get back to full fitness and top form. The club expected to win trophies every year, in Spain and in Europe, and that meant finding replacements if their top players weren't available.

That truth was in the back of Ousmane's mind while he went through another workout on the treadmill. The good news was that Barcelona had amazing facilities, and they took great care of him, including lots of reminders to make sure he was always there for his appointments. The bad news was that he still needed to get through a few more steps in the treatment plan before he could return to training with the rest of the squad. He prayed that he wouldn't have to wait much longer.

At last, he got the thumbs up from the doctors and physios. It had never felt so good to put on his training kit and tie up his boots.

'I'm Leo, nice to meet you,' Leo teased when he saw Ousmane ready to join their practice drill before practice started.

Ousmane laughed. 'Oh come on – I haven't been away for that long!' he shot back.

'Use that frustration as extra motivation,' Antoine added. 'We've really missed you, but you're back in time for some big games.'

Ousmane nodded. He had been reading the fixture list so carefully that he knew it by heart. Big games were nice but, after missing so much time, he would settle for any game, really.

CHAPTER 21

CONVINCING CAMP NOU

'Dembélé! Dembélé! Dembélé!' the Barcelona fans chanted and cheered while Ousmane warmed up near the touchline.

What a beautiful sound! There was nothing like a packed Camp Nou crowd. He looked up to see rows of fans standing and clapping.

The league title celebrations on the pitch in the summer of 2019 felt a long, long time ago to Ousmane. Since then, he had spent more time on the treatment table than on the pitch, and no one was more disappointed about that than him.

But he was finally fit again – and this time, he was determined that it would last.

'It's a fresh start,' he told Xavi, the latest Barcelona

boss. 'That's the way I'm thinking about it. It's been so frustrating, but I've got to look forward now. There's no point thinking about the last few years.'

The true Barcelona fans hadn't given up on Ousmane. They had seen flashes of his dribbling magic, and they had seen enough superstars over the years to recognise what this young winger could become. The big question was: Could he get back to doing that every week?

A lot had changed at the club since the last time Ousmane pulled on the Barca shirt. Leo had moved to PSG, but there was still plenty of talent in this squad, with Sergio Busquets, Frenkie de Jong and teenage midfielder Pedri.

Then another friendly face arrived halfway through the season. Ousmane's phone pinged with a new text.

'Guess who's coming to Barca?!'

It was Auba. Ousmane rushed to reply, then checked the news online. Sure enough, there was a report about Barcelona signing Pierre-Emerick Aubameyang, Ousmane's old Dortmund pal.

That put an even bigger smile on Ousmane's face.

Auba was such a fun character in the dressing room and a deadly finisher on the pitch. He had a good feeling about this season.

Ousmane was feeling more settled off the pitch too. He had a girlfriend called Rima, who brought more balance to his life and helped him switch off after training or games. Football didn't have to be at the centre of everything all the time.

On the pitch, he was doing what he did best – dribbling, spinning defenders inside out and making the right pass. He finished the season with thirteen assists, the most in the league.

At times, he still thought about the injuries. But he trusted all the work he had done with the physios and doctors. He was stronger now, and there wasn't the same fear every time he tripped or slipped. He could get into top gear in his sprints without holding anything back.

That carried over into the 2022–23 season too. There was a youthful buzz around the club, and Ousmane was excited to team up with new striker Robert Lewandowski, who they all called Lewy.

Lewy gave Ousmane a great target for crosses and through balls, and they were soon working on that connection in training.

Ousmane also wanted to make some improvements on his personal goal tally. Sometimes he would get into great positions and rush the shot, or take an extra touch when he didn't need it. But hours of preseason shooting practice eventually paid off.

Against Inter Milan, he timed his run into the box perfectly, thumping a shot past the keeper.

Gooooooooooooooooooooooaaaaaaaaaaaaaaaaaaa aaaaaaalllllllllllllllllllllllllllll!

He was on the attack again against Athletic Bilbao when Frenkie's pass put him one-on-one with a defender. There was only the tiniest gap to aim for at the keeper's near post, but Ousmane unleashed a shot that flew into the top corner.

Gooooooooooooooooooooooaaaaaaaaaaaaaaaaaaa aaaaaaalllllllllllllllllllllllllllll!

It suited Ousmane that Barcelona were playing a little faster these days, instead of the slower buildups with lots of short passes. He had gradually adapted to that style, but he was still at his most dangerous when they launched lightning counterattacks, and he could get on the end of through balls.

In some ways, it was a shame that Ousmane and his teammates had to hit pause on the Barca season and switch their attention to the 2022 World Cup, which had been scheduled in November and December to avoid the summer heat in Qatar. As defending champions, France would have a pack of teams chasing them this time – but Ousmane wasn't going to let that faze him.

CHAPTER 22

A WORLD CUP ROLLERCOASTER: PART II

Ousmane was full of his usual energy and excitement when he met up with Coach Deschamps and the rest of the France squad. He just hoped he had brought his Barcelona form with him. His bad injury luck hadn't just made it tough to get going at Barca – it had cut down on his chances to play for France too. From now on, he was going to appreciate these tournaments even more.

'There's nothing like the World Cup vibes,' he said to Kylian as they walked through the team's hotel.

'It's the biggest stage of all,' Kylian agreed. 'So we've got to do everything possible to keep hold of the trophy!'

Ousmane wasn't just back in the France squad. He was back in the team, starting in the front four with Kylian, Antoine and Olivier. With solid defenders and midfielders behind him, Ousmane had the freedom he loved. France ripped through Group D, then brushed Poland aside in the next round.

'All I can say to opposition defenders is good luck!' Olivier joked. 'They've got to deal with Kylian on one wing and Ousmane on the other!'

After wins over England and Morocco, France were heading for another World Cup final – and this time it was against Leo and Argentina.

Four years ago, Ousmane had been watching the final from the bench, cheering on his teammates. This time, he was starting on the right wing and getting the full sense of what it meant to play in football's biggest game.

Ousmane did most of his early work in his own half, helping his defenders and closing down the Argentina midfielders. Then he ended up in the right-back position, trying to block a cross from Argentina winger Ángel Di María. Except Di María didn't swing in a cross. Just like Ousmane loved to do at the other end of the pitch, he faked a cross and dribbled into the box instead.

As Ousmane sprinted to catch up, he stretched to make a tackle. Di María ended up on the floor and Ousmane got a sinking feeling when he heard the referee's whistle. Penalty to Argentina!

Nooooooooo!

Ousmane put his arms in the air. 'I didn't touch him!' he pleaded to the referee. His teammates couldn't believe it either.

Leo scored the penalty, and Di María added a second goal fifteen minutes later.

Ousmane was stunned. But before he could even think about sparking a comeback, he saw the electronic board on the touchline, and the referee signalled for a substitution. Coach Deschamps wasn't waiting until half-time to make some changes. He was subbing off Ousmane and Olivier now.

Oh dear! Ousmane's head was spinning as he walked off the pitch. His World Cup final was over after just forty-one minutes. He understood that Coach

Deschamps needed to change things to find a way back into the game, but it still stung. Ousmane was a proud competitor, and nothing could have prepared him for this nightmare first half.

'This wasn't about anything you did,' Coach Deschamps explained. 'I needed to change the formation while there was still time.'

A late France comeback got Ousmane smiling again, but he could only watch as Argentina won the penalty shootout. If he had been on the pitch, he might have taken one of the penalties. That was one of the many thoughts running through his head while he watched the Argentina players celebrating at the far end of the pitch.

Eventually, he found Leo in the sea of players, coaches and photographers. As much as Ousmane was hurting, he wanted to congratulate his friend. When they were together at Barcelona, Leo had talked a few times about what it would mean to finally win the World Cup for his country.

'Congratulations, champ,' Ousmane said, hugging Leo. 'You deserved it today.'

DEMBÉLÉ

'Thanks, man,' Leo replied. 'Keep your head up. You'll be back in the final again. I know it.'

It would take some time for Ousmane to stop thinking about the penalty and the early substitution, but he also had some great memories from the 2022 World Cup. He had proved himself as a regular starter in Coach Deschamps' attack, and his body had responded well to some tense, physical matches.

There was no time to dwell on the ups and downs, though. Coach Xavi had already contacted all the Barcelona players about the plan for returning to training, and Ousmane was soon putting on his boots again, with the rest of the season just around the corner.

CHAPTER 23

CHAMPIONS AGAIN

'Back to business, baby!' Ousmane shouted while he jogged over to the training pitch, giving Coach Xavi a fist bump on the way.

It was a strange feeling. The Barcelona players were going through a mini preseason, but they had already played fourteen league games before the World Cup break.

The first test was the Spanish Super Cup against Real Madrid in January. Any game against their big rivals was fiery enough already, and this time there was a trophy up for grabs. It didn't take long for the crunching tackles to fly in, but Ousmane was quick enough to dodge them, and Barcelona got the upper hand in a 3–1 win.

DEMBÉLÉ

'Keep playing our way,' Coach Xavi urged his players. 'If we do that, the wins will keep piling up.'

Every week, someone different stepped up for Barca. One game, it was Lewy. The next, it was Raphinha or Gavi or Frenkie.

But Barcelona struggled to unlock the Real Sociedad defence in the Spanish Cup quarter-final. Then Ousmane burst free down the right wing and got in front of his marker. With one strong touch, he powered into the penalty area. Lewy was in the box for a cross, but Ousmane went for glory, thundering a shot that caught the keeper by surprise.

Gooooooooooooooooooooooaaaaaaaaaaaaaaaaaaa aaaaaaalllllllllllllllllllllllllllll!

Ousmane leapt into the air by the corner flag as the Camp Nou crowd roared.

'I was about to complain that you didn't pass it, but then you did *that*!' Lewy joked. 'What a hit!'

Even while Barcelona stormed to victory after victory, none of the players wanted to jinx anything by talking about the league table. But they were all thinking about it, especially as they extended their lead at the top. The club hadn't won the Spanish league since 2019, and no one needed to remind the Barca fans about the disappointments of the last few years.

Whenever Ousmane saw a group of supporters in the street that season, he heard the same thing.

'Bring that trophy back home where it belongs, Ousmane!' they said.

'That's the plan!' he always replied. So far, the plan was working.

As the Barcelona squad travelled to face local rivals Espanyol, the maths had become simple. A win would seal the Spanish league title.

'Let's finish the job, boys!' Ousmane called out in the dressing room while the clock ticked down towards kick-off.

'Don't expect this to be easy,' Coach Xavi added. 'Be ready for a tough game, because Espanyol will be trying to spoil our party.'

Barcelona raced to a 4–2 win, but there would be no party that afternoon. As Ousmane and his teammates raised their arms into the air at the final whistle, some angry Espanyol fans rushed onto the pitch. The Barcelona players noticed just in time.

'Quick, guys!' Ousmane called as they sprinted back down the tunnel and into the safety of the dressing room.

The actual trophy party came at Camp Nou after the next game – and there were big smiles everywhere, even though Barca had lost to Real Sociedad fifteen minutes earlier.

It had been a very long season, with the World Cup wedged in the middle, but Ousmane didn't care as he picked up the trophy, kissed it and lifted it proudly. This joy was what it was all about!

'Campeones, Campeones! Olé! Olé! Olé!' they all sang, with the coaches joining the scrum of people on the stage. All the Barcelona supporters had stayed in their seats after the game. No one wanted to miss the celebrations.

'This never gets old,' Ousmane said, hugging Coach Xavi as they walked around the pitch and waved to the fans. 'We're number one again!'

'Tell me about it!' Coach Xavi replied, smiling. 'I won

a lot of trophies here as a Barcelona player, but I'm still getting emotional today!'

At last, Ousmane could look forward to some holiday time to rest his aching body. 'I think we've earned it!' he said to himself with a grin.

While he and Rima got ready to catch up with family and friends that summer, it was nice to hit pause on the football world – for a few weeks, at least.

CHAPTER 24

COMING HOME

Even though Ousmane had been playing in Germany and Spain for the past seven seasons, France still felt like home. Whether he was visiting family and friends in Évreux or joining up with the French squad for an international match, there was something special about seeing familiar faces and special places.

But even though his friends always tried to persuade him to come back for good, he hadn't thought about returning to the French league until he started to hear rumours about PSG being interested in him. Now he was really confused about what to do.

'I feel like I've got unfinished business at Barca,' he told his mum while he was trying to sort through his feelings. 'I want to win the Champions League here. I want to keep playing for these great fans. But PSG was such a big part of my childhood, and there would be something really cool about coming back to France.'

'Well, can you have a meeting with PSG to learn more about their plans for the future?' Fatimata asked. 'It sounds like you need to find out more. Once you've met with them, I'm sure you'll have a clearer idea about what to do.'

Ousmane agreed. That was the best thing to do. They arranged the meeting with PSG – and the conversation went even better than Ousmane had expected.

'We're looking ahead to the next version of our team,' they explained. 'We want the best French talent to be playing here. Kylian is here, and you're the perfect co-star to lead us forward.'

Travelling back to Barcelona, Ousmane daydreamed about scoring spectacular goals. But in those dreams, he wasn't wearing a Barca shirt. He was wearing a PSG shirt.

He had made up his mind. He wanted the next chapter of his career to happen in Paris. When PSG came in with an offer, Barcelona knew it was time to move on.

'I come from Évreux, not far from here,' Ousmane explained to the media once the transfer was official. 'The world talks about Paris Saint-Germain, and I think I was destined to sign for this club one day.'

There had been some ups and downs in Barcelona, but Ousmane preferred to remember all the good times. He had won three Spanish league titles and two Spanish cups while playing with some of the best players in the world.

But his future was with PSG, playing in attack with Kylian.

'Not bad!' Moustapha told him. 'First, Lionel Messi. Now, Kylian Mbappé. You know how to end up with great teammates!'

Ousmane laughed. 'We're going to score some incredible goals,' he said. 'Just think about the counterattacks. Defenders are going to be left in the dust!'

He got an even bigger buzz when PSG gave him the Number 10 shirt. For the second time in his career,

Ousmane was stepping into Neymar's shoes. The Brazilian star had left Paris to join the Saudi league, and there were other changes at the club too. Luis Enrique had been named as the new PSG manager, and he and Ousmane had some great conversations about how the team would play.

Ousmane had taken a while to get going in Barcelona, but he made a flying start for PSG. Against Monaco at the Parc des Princes, he sprinted down the right wing and controlled a long pass with a perfect touch that gave his marker no chance of intercepting it. He raced clear into the box and crashed a thunderous shot past the keeper at the near post.

Gooooooooooooooooooooooaaaaaaaaaaaaaaaaaaa aaaaaaalllllllllllllllllllllllllll!

His new teammates raced over to celebrate with him, led by Kylian, Achraf Hakimi and Gonçalo Ramos. Ousmane jumped in the air, firing up the PSG fans in that corner of the stadium. He had officially arrived!

But the biggest games of his first season in Paris came in the Champions League, when PSG were drawn against Barcelona in the quarter-finals.

DEMBÉLÉ

'I know my way around Camp Nou, at least,' Ousmane joked. 'I'm not sure all the fans will give me a warm welcome, though!'

Overall, he was calm about it, and he let his feet do the talking in the first leg. With PSG trailing 1–0, he raced forward and sent Kylian free down the left wing. Kylian's cross was cleared straight to Ousmane, who calmly faked a right-footed shot, then slipped the ball across his body to use his left foot instead. He saw a tiny gap and didn't hesitate, firing a shot into the top corner.

Gooooooooooooooooooooooaaaaaaaaaaaaaaaaaaa aaaaaaalllllllllllllllllllllllllllll!

Barcelona still came away with a 3–2 win, and there were some disappointed faces in the PSG dressing room. But Ousmane saw it differently.

'We matched them for most of the game, and we can find another gear in the second leg,' he said, clapping his hands. 'There's still a lot of football left. It's not over yet.'

Even so, Barcelona scored first in the second leg, leaving PSG with a mountain to climb.

'Time for some magic,' Ousmane said to Kylian as they waited for a throw-in.

A Barcelona red card opened the door for PSG, and Ousmane helped to barge through it. When a low cross fizzed into the box, Ousmane stretched for a first-time shot. He connected with power, sending it past the keeper before he could move.

Goooooooooooooooooooooaaaaaaaaaaaaaaaaaaa aaaaaaalllllllllllllllllllllllllllll!

'Yes!' he shouted. 'Get the ball. Let's go!'

The noise from the Barcelona fans got even quieter when Vitinha drilled in a long range shot. 4–4 on aggregate.

'We're on top now!' Ousmane called. 'Don't sit back. Keep attacking!'

Ousmane pushed forward again and got to the ball first, just before a crunching Barca tackle sent him tumbling to the floor. As he fell, Ousmane heard the referee's whistle. Penalty!

Kylian hammered it in, then added another in the final minutes.

'What a comeback!' Ousmane shouted, jumping on

DEMBÉLÉ

Kylian's back in front of the PSG fans who had made the trip to Spain.

Ousmane was used to celebrations in the home dressing room at Camp Nou, but this time, the party was in the away dressing room, on a legendary night for PSG.

Their Champions League run came up short, but Ousmane was soon celebrating with the French league trophy. It was even more special to know that so many of his friends were watching that day.

The French cup final against Lyon was a chance for him to add another trophy to his collection in his first season in Paris, and he knew his teammates were counting on him for a big performance.

When left-back Nuno Mendes controlled a pass on the left wing, Ousmane sensed his chance. He sprinted to the back post and was totally unmarked as the cross landed on his head. He wasn't always the best at headers, but there was no way he was missing this one.

Gooooooooooooooooooooooaaaaaaaaaaaaaaaaaaaaaaaaaalllllllllllllllllllllllllllll!

That set PSG on the way to a 2–1 win, and Ousmane was still buzzing from the celebrations as he packed his bags in preparation for Euro 2024. Maybe, just maybe, there would be even more trophies ahead that summer.

CHAPTER 25

EUROS MAGIC

'With this squad, we've always got a good chance,' Ousmane explained, as more and more microphones appeared in front of him. After his performances alongside Kylian for PSG, France fans had high hopes for that pairing at Euro 2024.

Coach Deschamps had the same idea. 'Ousmane, you'll be starting on the right wing,' he explained. 'But you, Kylian and Antoine can switch positions to confuse defenders.'

Despite all the star power, the French attack stumbled during the group stage. It took an own goal to beat Austria 1–0 , and a penalty to draw with Poland. Perhaps it was the long league season, but things weren't clicking. There were lots of suggestions floating around in the team meetings:

'We need to move the ball faster.'
'We're not getting the ball into the box enough.'
'We have to use the wings more.'

Ousmane agreed with all of that. Hopefully, they were just saving their best form for the knockout rounds.

But it was a similar story in the quarter-finals against Portugal. Ousmane was on the bench that day, but Coach Deschamps turned to him for a spark in the second half.

'We need more pace out there,' he told Ousmane. 'Get on the ball and drive us forward. We've got to give their defenders something to worry about.'

Ousmane liked the sound of that. He passed on the message about moving the ball faster, and he stayed close to the touchline to give himself extra space. When he got the ball, he was decisive, making defenders back off and setting up two chances that his teammates fired wide.

Suddenly, every attack was flowing through Ousmane. Portugal looked terrified to put in a tackle,

DEMBÉLÉ

and he glided forward into dangerous positions. When he was in this kind of mood, he made the game look so easy.

'The goal is coming!' he yelled, clapping and trying to transfer some of his energy to the rest of the team.

But he was wrong. Neither team could score, and the game went to penalties.

Ousmane huddled together with his teammates, as Coach Deschamps praised their hard work and looked for penalty takers for the shootout.

'I'll take one,' Ousmane said without hesitation.

Coach Deschamps nodded. 'Okay, you go first,' he replied.

Ousmane picked up the ball and placed it carefully on the spot. He took a deep breath, then five steps backwards and a little skip to his left. He knew where he wanted to hit it, but he didn't want to give the keeper any clues.

He ran up, watching the Portugal keeper all the way. When he saw the keeper start his dive to the right, Ousmane placed the ball into the opposite corner.

'Yes!!' he yelled, then he ran over to hug France keeper Mike Maignan. 'You've got this, big man!'

He rejoined his teammates on the halfway line, getting a high-five from everyone.

'Nicely done, Dembouz!' they called, all sounding a little tense.

Now he could only watch. The next four penalties flew into the net, then a Portugal miss gave France the advantage. When Theo Hernández scored the winning penalty, Ousmane raced over to join the celebrations, jumping onto the pile. None of them cared that France had wasted good chances and failed to score in 120 minutes. They were into the semi-finals – that was all that mattered.

The night got even better for Ousmane when he was named Man of the Match. He stood with the trophy and smiled, but inside he was just thinking about getting some rest. Even though he hadn't played the whole game, he had given everything and he was exhausted, physically and mentally.

Ousmane was back in the team for the semi-final against Spain, and he was dreaming of another major final when France took an early lead. But the night ended in despair as Spain fought back to win 2–1, inspired by a wonder goal from Lamine Yamal.

It took Ousmane a few days to shake off the disappointment. He was used to getting to big finals with France, and it hurt to fall short this time. But there was always another game ahead and another trophy to chase.

By the time he was back in Paris, though, there were soon other things on Ousmane's mind.

CHAPTER 26

THE 'FALSE NINE' AND THE TREBLE QUEST

The news shook everyone. Ousmane stared at the TV screen. 'Wow!' he said.

Kylian was leaving PSG to join Real Madrid. The rumours had been floating around for months, but now there was no doubt about it.

'He's really leaving,' Ousmane said, turning up the volume and listening to all the details. He had tried not to distract Kylian during the Euros with talk about his future, but now it had become the biggest sports news story. The main TV presenter was calling it the end of an era for PSG.

Ousmane was sad that his partnership with Kylian wouldn't continue next season, but he was happy for his friend. He understood that it was a dream move, and he knew that he had been in that position himself in the past.

In the space of a few years, PSG had lost Neymar, Leo and Kylian. So it didn't take long for a different angle to develop. After all the big-name departures, reporters in Paris were now calling Ousmane the main man.

Looking around the dressing room, that wasn't quite true, even if everyone wanted to call him that. There was still a lot of talent, with players ready to step into bigger roles and a brighter spotlight. Ousmane was one of them, but PSG also had Vitinha, Achraf, João Neves, Fabián Ruiz, Doué and captain Marquinhos, who had been at the club forever.

Coach Enrique was equally positive as the squad prepared for the 2024–25 season.

'This is why we signed you, Ousmane,' he said. 'I've seen the way you've grown as a player over the last few years, and we're going to rely on you even more now.'

Everything in Ousmane's career so far had been leading up to this moment. He could see that now.

He was older, he set a strong example – and he had become a father, which brought extra responsibilities.

'If you're willing to work that hard, others will follow,' he remembered his Évreux coaches telling him. It had been true then, and it was true now at the highest level.

It didn't matter what anyone else was saying about this PSG squad. The belief was there in the dressing room. Everyone had a job to do and, together, they could make up for the talent they had lost.

Before long, all the talk about PSG taking a step back gave the players extra motivation. They had never been a one-man team when Kylian was at his very best. They had never been a three-man team when they had Leo and Neymar alongside him. So why did no one want to believe in PSG as a Champions League contender anymore? They just needed to get a little creative – and that's exactly what Coach Enrique did.

Ousmane had spent his whole career as a winger or an attacking midfielder, getting into positions to dribble, take on defenders and whip in crosses. So he wasn't sure what to say when Coach Enrique explained a new role that he wanted to try. The 'false nine'.

'You'll start as a central striker, but with the freedom to drop deep, drift to the left or the right, and that will create some difficult questions for the centre-backs,' he explained. 'When you pull them out of position, it opens up space for everyone else.'

'But then we'll have no one in the box,' Ousmane said, trying to picture what it would look like on the pitch if they had three wingers and no strikers.

'That's where midfield runs are so important,' Coach Enrique continued. 'Plus, you'll swap positions with the wingers sometimes and they'll be further forward. Maybe, we just need to see it in action, but it should mean even more scoring chances for you.'

Ousmane nodded. He remembered how Leo had played that type of role for Barcelona, and he was happy to give it a try. The PSG coaches created drills to practice the false nine movements in training, where Ousmane was marked by Marquinhos. That helped him learn where to be and how he could open up gaps by pulling out to the wings and making runs from deeper positions.

The results were instant:

A hat-trick against Stuttgart

A hat-trick against Stade Brest

Two more goals against Monaco

'Should we be offended that no one thinks we have any stars anymore?' Ousmane asked, laughing. 'We still seem pretty good!'

This one tactical change had pushed PSG to a new level – and none of it worked without Ousmane's all-round quality. He was stepping up in the Champions League too. When PSG lost the first leg at home to Liverpool in the Last 16, there was still a quiet confidence in the dressing room. Somehow, Liverpool had won 1–0, even though Ousmane and his teammates combined for twenty-seven shots.

'We'll shoot better in the second leg,' Ousmane said.

It wouldn't be easy to turn things around at Anfield. Liverpool were so good at home, but Ousmane believed they could do it. He started a counterattack with a pass to the wing, then he sprinted into the box, pointing to where he wanted the ball. As the cross came in, Ousmane stretched for it, and the Liverpool keeper collided with a defender. Ousmane pounced on the rebound for a tap-in.

Goooooooooooooooooooooooaaaaaaaaaaaaaaaaaaa aaaaaaalllllllllllllllllllllllllllll!

'There we go, boys!' he shouted. 'Let's do this!'

It was another example of Ousmane being a leader. With one quick move, he had given PSG real hope. When the game went to a penalty shootout, Ousmane still felt good, especially with giant Gianluigi Donnarumma in goal for PSG.

Sure enough, Donnarumma made the difference, and Ousmane took his penalty with a typically calm run-up. The connection felt good as he struck the ball, and he watched it fly into the net. Doué smashed in the winning penalty, and PSG had passed their biggest test so far.

'Here we come!' Ousmane shouted, celebrating with the away fans. The Champions League highlights continued against Aston Villa and Arsenal, sending

PSG through to the final.

They wrapped up the French league and cup double, and the attention turned to the Champions League again – the prize they wanted most of all.

'Winning the French league and cup is great, but winning the Champions League would be historic for PSG,' Ousmane said as he and Vitinha warmed up at Allianz Arena, ready for the big game. 'Can you imagine the parties in Paris?!'

As Coach Enrique walked down the touchline before kick-off, he knew there was nothing more he could do. He had given his players one last message, and now it was up to them to deliver against Inter in the final. There would probably be some nerves, but they just had to keep battling, even if things weren't going their way.

But that night in Germany, everything went PSG's way in the most dominant European final performance ever. Ousmane set up two goals in a 5–0 win, and the long wait was finally over. PSG had won the Champions League at last!

It was the perfect performance to end a spectacular

season. Ousmane had played the best football of his career, and the French league's Player of the Year award was another nice surprise. He had become one of the main men for PSG, and he had the trophies to prove it.

CHAPTER 27

CHASING NEW GOALS

Ousmane got up from the sofa and groaned. His body was still sore. He had played so much football over the past year. But the non-stop football calendar listed the upcoming FIFA Club World Cup as the next big target.

'The games never end!' Fatimata said in amazement when she heard about this latest tournament.

Ousmane grinned and shrugged. He had already made up his mind – he wanted to be there, and he wanted to win another trophy. So he was soon boarding the plane with his teammates and travelling to the USA.

PSG would have to handle some scorching hot summer weather, and the water bottles were lined up around the pitch in training. Ousmane sat out the early games, but he was back to face Real Madrid in the semi-finals.

'We can send a message today, boys,' Ousmane said in the dressing room.

'That's right,' Achraf added. 'Let's show everyone that PSG are the new kings of Europe.'

They sent that message in the loudest way possible. In the opening minutes, Ousmane was too quick for a Real Madrid defender and Fabián Ruiz tapped in the loose ball. Then Ousmane punished another Real Madrid mistake, racing through and curling a shot into the bottom corner.

Goooooooooooooooooooooooaaaaaaaaaaaaaaaaaaaa aaaaaaalllllllllllllllllllllllllllll!

PSG were having a party. Achraf ran over and pretended to shine Ousmane's boots, and the score was soon 3–0 as that duo combined to set up Fabián Ruiz for his second goal.

It wasn't quite at the level of their 5–0 Champions League final performance, but it was close. Real Madrid looked stunned.

Although PSG lost to Chelsea in the Club World

Cup final, Ousmane looked back proudly on a season that had felt like one long dream. On top of all the team success, he was also being mentioned as a favourite for the Ballon d'Or, just as Mikaël Silvestre had predicted years ago at Rennes.

'Winning the Ballon d'Or would be amazing,' Ousmane admitted. 'That's one of the biggest awards in the game, and I'm going to keep doing what I do.'

It hadn't always been easy, with injuries and disappointments to overcome, but Ousmane had battled his way to the top of the football mountain. The view from the top was pretty great, and he was going to do everything possible to stay there.

Borussia Dortmund
🏆 DFB-Pokal: 2016–17

Barcelona
🏆 La Liga: 2017–18, 2018–19, 2022–23
🏆 Copa Del Rey: 2017–18, 2020–21
🏆 Spanish Super Cup: 2018, 2023

PSG
🏆 Ligue 1: 2023–24, 2024–25
🏆 Coupe de France: 2023–24, 2024–25
🏆 French Super Cup: 2023, 2024
🏆 UEFA Champions League: 2024–25

France
🏆 FIFA World Cup: 2018

Individual
🏆 Ligue 1 Young Player of the Year: 2015–16
🏆 Bundesliga Rookie of the Season: 2016–17
🏆 Bundesliga Team of the Season: 2016–17
🏆 Ligue 1 Player of the Year: 2024–25
🏆 Ligue 1 Top Goalscorer (Joint): 2024–25
🏆 UEFA Champions League Player of the Season: 2024–25

DEMBÉLÉ

10 THE FACTS

NAME: Masour Ousmane Dembélé
DATE OF BIRTH: 15 May 1997
PLACE OF BIRTH: Vernon, France
NATIONALITY: French
BEST FRIENDS: Kylian Mbappé and Achraf Hakimi
CURRENT CLUB: PSG
SHIRT NUMBER: 10
POSITION: LW, RW, F

THE STATS

Height (cm):	178
Club appearances:	359
Club goals:	103
Club assists:	97
Club trophies:	15
International appearances:	56
International goals:	7
International trophies:	1
Ballon d'Ors:	0

★ ★ ★ **HERO RATING: 88** ★ ★ ★

GREATEST MOMENTS

 **6 MARCH 2016, RENNES 4–1 NANTES**

Ousmane had already shown flashes of his talent, but this was the day that he announced himself as a star. With an electric first-half hat-trick, he sent the Rennes fans into a frenzy and left the Nantes defenders with nightmares. Then his post-game interview made him an online sensation.

26 APRIL 2017, BAYERN MUNICH 2–3 BORUSSIA DORTMUND

This veteran Bayern Munich team didn't get rattled easily, but they had no answer for Ousmane in this cup semi-final. His inch-perfect cross set up Pierre-Emerick Aubameyang for the equaliser, before his wonderstrike silenced the Allianz Arena and sent Dortmund into the final. Not for the last time, Ousmane delivered when it mattered most.

11 DECEMBER 2018, BARCELONA 1–1 TOTTENHAM

The Camp Nou crowd got a taste of the Dembélé dynamo with a stunning solo goal that turned a Tottenham mistake into a 1–0 lead. Setting off inside his own half, this was Ousmane at his best, sprinting, dribbling and leaving defenders on the floor before finding the net. After all his injury misery, this wonder goal was even sweeter!

5 JULY 2024, FRANCE 0–0 PORTUGAL (FRANCE WIN 5–3 ON PENALTIES)

France couldn't score in this Euro 2024 quarter-final, or during the whole tournament really, but Ousmane brought the game to life as a second-half substitute. He kept his cool in the shootout, setting the tone by scoring the first penalty, and he walked away with the Man of the Match award.

31 MAY 2025, PSG 5–0 INTER MILAN

With two assists, countless clever touches and relentless pressing, Ousmane did a bit of everything to make this a historic night for PSG. His big target when he signed for the club was to bring the Champions League trophy to Paris, and they did it in style. Mission accomplished!

TEST YOUR KNOWLEDGE

QUESTIONS

1. What was the name of the building where Ousmane grew up?

2. How old was Ousmane when he joined ALM Évreux?

3. During his childhood, Ousmane's favourite Premier League players were David Beckham and which other midfielder?

4. Against which French league rival did Ousmane score a first-half hat-trick for Rennes?

5. Against which country did Ousmane make his France senior team debut?

6. True or False: Ousmane won the German Cup in his one season with Borussia Dortmund.

7. What was the transfer fee (in €) when Barcelona signed Ousmane?

8. True or False: Ousmane wore the Number 10 shirt for Barcelona.

9. Against which team was Ousmane named Man of the Match at Euro 2024?

10. What was the score when PSG beat Inter Milan in the 2025 Champions League final?

Answers below... No cheating!

1. La Madeleine; 2. Seven; 3. Steven Gerrard; 4. Nantes; 5. Italy; 6. True; 7. €105 million; 8. False (he wore the Number 10 shirt for PSG); 9. Portugal; 10. 5–0.

PLAY LIKE YOUR HEROES

PLAY LIKE YOUR HEROES
DRIBBLE LIKE DEMBÉLÉ

STEP 1: You're a speedy winger, born to entertain. First, get yourself into space to receive the ball and be aware of what's around you. If a defender is marking you tightly, fake to sprint one way, then duck back in the opposite direction.

STEP 2: Get the ball under control. You can't go anywhere if you leave that behind! Then drive forward, with confident touches, keeping the ball close to your feet so you can dodge any tackles.

STEP 3: Be ready to use either foot. Depending on where your teammates are, and how the defenders are positioned, you might either cut inside or push the ball to the outside. Use your judgement to choose whichever option will keep the nearest defender off balance.

STEP 4: Dip into your bag of tricks – a stepover, an elástico, or just a shoulder shimmy. But don't slow down. The skills are scarier when you're still running with pace.

STEP 5: Make this chance count. The defender is probably begging for you to get too excited and rush it. Take another glance at what's going on in the penalty area, then whip the ball in. If you've got it right, one of your teammates is about to get a goalscoring chance on a plate. If you're going it alone, make sure you test the keeper with your shot.

STEP 6: GOAL! Whether you've scored it yourself or set it up for someone else, make sure you celebrate in style with a big smile on your face.

CAN'T GET ENOUGH OF
ULTIMATE FOOTBALL HEROES?

Check out heroesfootball.com
for quizzes, games, and competitions!

Plus join the Ultimate Football Heroes
Fan Club to score exclusive content and
be the first to hear about
new books and events.
heroesfootball.com/subscribe/